Six Summers

-A Memoir-

Vincent Tipre

The people, places, and events in this story are real.

First published by Dog Ear Publishing
4010 W. 86th Street, Ste H
Indianapolis, IN 46268
www.dogearpublishing.net

ISBN: 978-159858-412-7

This book is printed on acid-free paper.

Printed in the United States of America

This book is dedicated to Gene and Julie,
who showed me how to lead.

Sixsummers.com

Acknowledgements

I want to thank my friends and family for their unwavering support, and proofreading. Your motivation kept me going.

Finally, for anyone that has ever worked or played at The Park, you are the heart and soul of this one.

Prologue

I consider myself to be one of the lucky ones. I just realized this. I have already found myself when so many others spend their entire lives searching.

As a kid growing up in Chicago, I spent most of my days across the street at the neighborhood park. When I was a kid I called this place Independence. Ah, how certain places or people can transcend the elementary names that our forefathers have provided. The Park is a title all in its own, a proper noun that has never spoken one word but has offered lifetimes of advice. Since kindergarten, life after school consisted of playing football, basketball, and baseball. I would unload my backpack and other belongings, pick up a ball, and race over to the nearest open field to play catch. Half of the time I didn't have company so I would just pretend to be Jerry Rice or Magic Johnson and conduct a verbal play by play of championship games and last second shots for hours upon hours. Some days I missed curfew and my mom would have to call me home from the front porch, "Vincent, time for dinner!" Going to The Park after school and on weekends was something I always looked forward to. A way to escape the world of school and two older brothers.

The summers were different at Independence. Every summer meant camp. The Park became so much more to me every June, a time when I could see old, almost-forgotten friends, and meet new ones to bond with, if only for a while. Day camp lasted just six weeks every year; still, it's hard for me to recall adolescent memories other than those from camp.

The years went by, I grew older and reached middle school, and my last years at camp dwindled down. As a twelve year old, my ambitions were changing. Namely, I wanted to exchange all my male friends with cute girls. But still, never for one day, did I ever turn into the camper who felt he was too old or too cool for camp.

Then, going into eighth grade, I turned thirteen and could no longer be a camper at Independence, but that couldn't be the end for me. I continued my summer routine and worked a few years as a counselor for The Park's Therapeutic Recreation camp. Finally, at the age of fifteen, I decided to apply for a position so I could be in charge of my own group. Consequently, the life I live today was set in motion by the six summers I spent working at The Park. Thirty-six amazing weeks that I wouldn't trade for the world. This was more than the best time of my life. The people, places, and things I encountered during my six years at Independence, in turn, became part of the maturation process that shaped the attitude and beliefs I currently hold. For that I am endlessly grateful.

Even more than family, I could count on The Park. It was just the right fit, like your favorite shirt - not the most expensive or colorful - but still the one you find yourself wearing the most.

I have been coming to The Park since I was four years old. Not just to swing on the swings but to be a part of it all: camp, tee ball, gymnastics, and the annual gym talent show. This place is my childhood. In the beginning, The Park was a place to hang out with friends and toss the ball around. Slowly it evolved into this living, screaming, running, and laughing entity that acted more as a friend than anything else. Sometimes at night, even now, I drive over to The Park and stop the car.

Endless memories fill my mind as I walk across the field and take a seat at the benches nearest the playground. The best tasting water in the world is from the drinking fountain over my right shoulder and the 'funball' field is to my left. Relax, breathe, smell, and remember it all.

June 2000

"So are we going to see if they are hiring over at The Park?" I questioned. Every day was the same during high school summer breaks from Lane Tech: Derek would come by my house and we would watch baseball and go swimming in my backyard. Today was different. Today we decided to get jobs.

"Yeah, let's go over there now and see if they have spots left," Derek replied. I watched him throw on his shoes and open my front door.

"I'm pretty sure that camp starts in like a week or two," I hastily explained as I threw on my shoes and tried to catch up with my already exiting friend. I had a job working for my dad at our family hardware store but decided I was in need of more stimulating work.

"Even if it starts tomorrow I'm down," Derek remarked. "As long as I can get some money. I mean, it seems like an okay job."

We walked towards the field house, the larger of the two buildings at Independence, taking in our surroundings. I wondered if the other edifice, the Women's Building, which was a smaller bungalow located on the southeast corner of The Park, was still home to the therapeutic camp, where I spent my last few summers working as a counselor. However, at a payment of five dollars a day, it was more like volunteering. "Well think about it this way. When I was a counselor I was stuck working in the Women's Building all day, struggling with most of the camper's disabilities, and making next to nothing…but I still loved it." I took it upon my self to convince him of The Park's high status. "I assume getting paid good money would make it even better."

A minute later we entered the field house. Almost immediately I had a smile on my face. I was shocked by the familiarity of it all: the dull, earthly tones of the main hallway, the rich chlorine smell wafting off of the pool, the echoing noises vibrating from the gymnasium. Whenever I think about The Park I am forced to smile. It amazed me that I had not thought to apply for a "real" summer job here before. Voices from the office caught our attention so we decided to take a look inside for someone to talk to about getting us some jobs.

Gene, The Park's supervisor, was standing in his office looking at some forms. As long as The Park has been in my life so has Gene. He was like an uncle to me. Growing up I feared him because of his intimidating size and rumored mean streak, but over the years he became a man I respected for his commitment to his job. I wasted no time in getting to the point. "Hey Gene, I was wondering if there are any rec. leader spots left for the summer."

He glanced at me and gave me a look of profound confusion, "Oh, it's you Tipre. What was your question, you want to be a rec. leader?"

"Yeah, I was wondering about it."

"This summer, like next week?" *Oh boy, game over.*

"Yeah, I know it's very late notice, but I figured to ask just in case."

"Well I actually have one open spot," he said, stepping past us and into the hallway, "but training is starting as we speak." It seemed like destiny was calling.

Gene stopped halfway to the gym and looked back at me. I thought about his words and hoped Derek would understand that I would take the one spot if Gene offered it to me. Still, I had envisioned a summer ruining children's lives with Derek by my side. "You really only have *one* spot?" I said back to Gene.

"Just the one," he reiterated, appearing now to finally understand that Derek was not just accompanying me on my job hunt but was also hoping to get hired. "You know that if your buddy wants the job too, I am going to offer it to you." He turned to Derek, "No offense, but Vince has been coming here year round since before I took over, and he has worked here as a counselor."

"Yeah, yeah, I definitely understand," he replied to Gene before facing me. "It's all yours," Derek said with a hint of disappointment.

I saw that Gene was ready to start the training session and wanted to know if I would be joining him in the gym. "Okay, do I come in the gym with you?" I said finally. I felt so awkward with Derek there, knowing that not only did he not get the job but also that he would have to go back and wait at my house for me.

"Yeah, we are starting now," Gene said. "You are sixteen, right?"

"I will be in the summer." I didn't notice a problem. Every year I was considered to be the age I turned during the summer. I recalled the year camp started and I was nine. Gene put me into the 10-12 year old age group because I would be ten in July. The cutoff was always the end of July.

Gene's facial expression lost its optimistic undertone, "The cutoff is the end of June. You have to be sixteen by the end of June to be even considered for a position." I wished his words were part of a joke, but they weren't. I was born five days too late to work. Derek, on the other hand, had been sixteen for months already.

"Are *you* sixteen?" Gene was now asking Derek.

"Yeah," he said nodding his head. He looked over at me with the same look I had just given him a minute before. "I would love to work here."

Gene looked at Derek and then back at me, "You vouch for him?" he asked honestly. It was nice that Gene wanted my input on the situation but I couldn't care less anymore.

"Yeah," I mumbled, still in disbelief over the recent change of events.

"Okay, well come into the gym now," I heard Gene say to Derek as I proceeded down the hallway for the door. "I will have you fill out the paperwork later." Gene didn't even know Derek's name but that didn't change the fact that he had just stolen my job from me. The walk back to my house was depressing, to say the least.

I ended up spending my summer with some friends from the neighborhood: my best friend Nick, his younger brother Stephen, and Stephen's two best friends, Dale and Frodo. Most days we would play whiffleball in Frodo's front yard and swim in Nick's pool. Once camp got out, everyday at four-thirty, Derek would make his way over to the rest of us. He would tell us stories about the kids at The Park and a girl he worked with, Katie.

"She's nineteen but I swear she flirts with me," Derek said one day.

"So ask her out," Nick advised.

"Didn't you hear me, she's nineteen," Derek reiterated. "But seriously guys, you have to meet her," Derek spoke like an agent for an A-list movie star. "She's funny and cute…you just have to meet her."

Everyday played out in pretty much the same manner. I slept late and sat around with the neighborhood guys and Derek hung out at night and talked about Katie. Without even meeting her one time, I felt like I got to know Katie fairly well that summer.

An old friend of mine, James, also had signed up to work at camp and once again became an important figure in my life. While we had known each other for nearly ten years already, James and I had a very strange relationship. Best friends for the two or three months each summer growing up, when day camp and baseball would link us, we would manage to lose touch annually right after James's birthday each August. Because of this, I was unsure how much I should be around the awkwardness that was new friend Derek and old friend James working together. It was only a matter of time until the two of them did not require my position as the middleman in their own friendship.

The days of summer wound down and camp ended. I had the same summer I always had, simple and fun, but Derek had new friends and memories when junior year began. After one summer of hearing about the greatest people, campers, bosses, and fun of his life, I was ready to suffocate Derek with his own teal day camp shirt.

With summer seeing its last days I had one goal in mind, to get a job at The Park nine months from now. I was going to be the greatest camp recreation leader the world had ever known. That and I would get paid to play games with eleven and twelve year olds all day.

I still wondered why this job was so important to me. Not only had I never even worked as a rec. leader one day in my life, there was the possibility that working at camp was nothing like the years I spent as a camper. Plus, sitting around and being a bum every previous summer was a blast. Nevertheless, The Park was calling to me as it had done for so many years of my life. Perhaps it was actually the persuasive voices of James and Derek, but regardless, I was drawn in to its powers and had been convinced that this was the job for me.

Year One

September '00

During the first of those grueling nine months of school, I made sure to remain in close contact with the two people in charge of day camp, Gene and Julie. Gene told me that as long as a spot opened up for next summer it was mine. Julie, the head instructor and day camp director, was one of my recreation leaders when I attended day camp. If Gene was my uncle, Julie was definitely my big sister. She was my big, happy sister, who would tell me cruel jokes and always treated me like I was more important than the other characters that passed through The Park's doors. Julie was the youngest twenty-seven year old in the world, and she was the biggest reason I wanted to work at The Park.

They say that junior year is supposed to be the toughest of the four. The last chance to boost your GPA before college applications are sent out first semester of senior year. Plus, preparing for the ACT exam, which would help stamp your fate after high school. I hate it when they are right.

"Room 404, where the hell is that?" With my eyes searching the room numbers of the fourth floor, I was certain that there was an error on my schedule. At least I had gained that upperclassman confidence, knowing that when I walked the halls of my high school, I knew where I was headed.

"Maybe it's in the *other* fourth floor section," Derek informed me, trying hard not to seem like a smart ass.

"Sir I'm serious…wait, is that a joke!? What do you mean 'other fourth floor section?'"

"Oh, well when I had music it was up the front stairwell, you know the ones by the main office. This part of the fourth floor isn't connected with that part."

"Really? That makes a lot of sense. Well I guess I'm going to head over that way then." I hustled off before anyone noticed that I was completely lost.

Apparently I didn't know everything there was to know about my high school. As the bell rang I realized that I was still making my way down the wrong fourth floor stairs. I hurried to find the ones leading back up to the correct fourth floor. *It is only the first day of class. No one would notice, let alone care, that I am late.* Then I saw the girl I was fonder of than anyone else on the planet, Leslie.

"Hey Vincenzo! What class are you going to?" I don't know why, but when she talked the simplest conversations seemed interesting to me.

"Music Appreciation," I said in a tone that was overly cool and collected. She seemed to notice a change in my tone and I attempted to cover it up with a throat-clearing cough. "I had no idea there were two separate fourth floors so I went up the wrong stairs."

"Yeah, that happened to me once too," she said, bringing some ease to the conversation. "I think back like freshman year." Rub it in.

"Well I'm already late…see ya," I said as I jogged off.

"Okay, bye," she called after me.

Ah Leslie. Half Puerto Rican, half Mexican, with an adorable face, a dancer's body, and a sense of humor that had made me cry on several occasions. She was also an insensitive, conceited, harsh, dimwitted, unappreciative pushover. That's how I knew she was the one for me. (I guess when you are sixteen you kind of allow yourself to fall victim to the traits that stand out at first glance. Everything else is blocked from your vision. If beer goggles are what you have on when you are drunk, then teen goggles are what you have on when you are in high school. Unfortunately, my pair blocked out the majority of Leslie's defining characteristics).

I showed up for class three minutes late but didn't care. Project Leslie had begun.

April '01

I didn't see much of James during junior year. He vanished the way he always did growing up. Derek and I met up with him a few times at The Park, where we would make use of my newly acquired driver's license and patrol the streets of northern Chicago in my 2000 red Mercury Mystique talking about next summer and how it will be the time of our lives. Then James would disappear for two more months. He was forever unavailable for someone who lived three blocks away, as though he had to drive in from out of town to see us.

When I wasn't working with my dad at our family hardware store after school, I was over at Nick's living the life. We went to different high schools so we only had limited time together, but we always seemed to be on the same page.

I was worried that having Derek around even more than before would lead to some issues. We were a tight knit group with particular routines but it never blossomed into a problem. Despite hanging out everyday, we never were without something to do. After school was dedicated to sports out on our front lawns and weekends to watching movies and taking trips to McDonald's. As much as I cherished the times when everyone was around, I started to favor days when Nick and Derek were busy. That left just me and the young guys.

Stephen, Frodo and Dale, who were all three or four years my junior, were the little brothers I never had. We managed to play sports and engage in important conversations at the same time. At least hold discussions about issues that were important to a group of middle school students. Basketball over at Frodo's house everyday became time for our family dinner conversation. I would tell them about my inability to speak to Leslie in complete sentences and they would talk about upcoming tests they were dreading or relationship drama with their friends. Many nights of playing basketball, Risk, and Magic the Gathering with the boys taught me a great deal about the kind of person I wanted to be. I enjoyed teaching Stephen and Frodo how to play defense on the basketball court or think a turn ahead in Magic, just as I loved it when Dale would come to me for advice about some girl at school. Originally, Stephen was just Nick's brother, and Frodo and Dale were simply Stephen's friends. That year I became close friends with all of them on my own. I felt completely content with my job, my friends, and my life.

Still, at the end of the day, The Park was always on my mind.

Nine months is a long time to wait for the perfect job, but my friends helped my toughest year come and go in a flash. I was really enjoying life, and for the first time was beginning to believe that everything was going to work out for me in the end. And then it did.

Day camp application time meant going over to Warren Park and filling out what felt like a hundred repetitive forms. Name. Social Security Number. Date. Past Experience. Name. Address. Phone Number. Social Security Number. Have you ever been convicted of a felony? If so, when? Date. Past Experience. Driver License Number. Address. Am I eligible to fill out the 1040-EZ? Job Title. Phone Number. Finally, as I thought my hand was going to fall off, I was done. Now, all I had to do was wait.

Who knew that anticipating a job related phone call could be more stressful than waiting for Leslie's number to appear on my caller I.D. So far, neither had happened. The school year was almost over and I began to panic. Derek, James, and twenty or so other Independence Park returning employees were already done with their processing months ago. It was the time when new employees would fill the remaining open positions left by the rec. leaders who had moved on. Why anyone under the age of forty would leave their six week long, nine dollar an hour job for anything else was beyond me.

Two weeks after my application was sent in, I stopped over at The Park to see if there was any news about my employment.

"Your name is on my list." Gene uttered nonchalantly to me. I guess someone who has run The Park for fifteen or so years no longer understands life-altering information such as this.

"Really! So I have a job?"

"No, your name is on the list of people I should specifi-cally not hire." Gene never was very funny.

"Okay, well what's the next step?"

"They will call and you'll have to go in to take the drug test. I assume your not going to fail that are you?"

"Drug test? Does that detect all the cocaine and heroine I have been using?" The blank expression on Gene's face told me that he did not appreciate, or simply did not understand my failed stab at humor. "Okay Gene, I'm gonna get going. When can I expect this call?"

"By the end of the month I would say."

"Okay, thanks a lot."

June '01

The end of junior year saw one successful urine test, the ACTs, three more failed conversations with Leslie, and train-ing day for camp. This day was usually held for rec. leaders and counselors on the Friday before the first week of camp. I would soon come to find out that it was more work and confusion than I ever could have imagined.

I showed up at The Park at a quarter to eleven for training. James and Derek were already there, in the gym shooting around, so I joined them. We had fifteen minutes to kill.

Most people thought Derek and I were brothers because we looked so similar. We are about the same height and build, but I think very distinguishable from each other, especially in personality. Derek is very low key. A witty philosopher with twelve-year-old interests. I am loud, aggressive, and talkative.

James is somewhat of a mix. He is a few inches shorter than me, five eleven to my six one. He complains about the girlfriend that he never sees, hates anyone he doesn't know, and loves being the funniest guy in the room.

We shot around for a few minutes before being requested by Julie to help setup tables and chairs on the court. Derek, James, and I were halfway done with the setup when the rec. leaders started to file in, and I began to feel out of place. Besides James and Derek, I only knew one other rec. leader, Becky. I had known her since we went to camp together as kids.

"Hey there," I said sitting in the chair across the table from her.

"Hi, Derek told me you were going to be working here this year. How are you?"

"Good, good. A little nervous about this whole process."

She looked towards the gym entry as a few more rec. leaders walked in. "Yeah, don't worry about it. You pretty much know day camp better than everyone here without even working a day. I was nervous last year, but after today, you'll be fine." Julie was passing out binders, clipboards, and stacks of information sheets to each table as Becky scanned our table for her group's stack. "Which group are you with?" she asked me, grabbing the binder for her girl's group.

"Actually, I'm not sure," I said, just now realizing I might get stuck with the youngest kids in play camp. "Be right back." I rose from my chair and maneuvered over to Derek who was talking with a rec. leader I didn't know.

"Hey Vince, this is someone I would like you to meet." Derek began to introduce me but she needed no introduction. Derek had talked about her constantly for the last year. I recognized her immediately from her red hair and cheerful attitude. Derek was right though, she was cute.

"Hi Katie."

"Hi Vince."

"Hey, when will I find out what group I have?" I asked them.

"Right now," Derek said turning his gaze towards Julie, who was now standing at the head of the tables.

We walked over to an open table and I searched my memory for names. I decided that picking out rec. leaders based on stories from Derek and James was a kind of game. Using what they had told me I could systematically eliminate people in order to name the rest. It didn't work very well. I was constantly asking Derek questions about the other employees, trying to tighten my search for other names and faces that might look familiar. I wanted to know whom he met last summer and who was new like me. He had just pointed out Cesar, a name I recognized, as Julie handed me a binder that said "9 & 10 year old boys" on it.

"Here Mr. Tipre, you and James are sharing this group," she said. James looked over at me and gave me a dorky thumbs up. *Nothing to worry about*, I thought to myself.

Amidst the random conversations now going on, Julie bombarded us with endless camper forms that had to be filled out, sorted alphabetically, and arranged in folders according to age and gender. Then, photocopies of rosters were printed, collected, re-written, re-printed, and finally put into binders that were going to become our own personal offices for the next six weeks.

I was told these binders would become the location of many letters from campers' parents regarding allergies, early dismissals, and reasons that swimming is "not in the best interest of our family." Pens and markers would be stored, lost, and found again days and even weeks later amongst the confusion of the binder. Emergency forms were exchanged between rec. leaders as children magically aged a year or two from when their parents filled out their date of birth two months before at registration. How a small binder, holding so much personal information, can be left in the hands of a six-teen-year-old is beyond me. I felt like a school nurse.

Training day was not just about meeting new people and organizing binders. It was also about meeting the lifeguards and going over their rules of the pool. James complained to me that these are the same lifeguards who all of last summer ate McDonald's while on duty, as fifty children were swim-ming in the pool. Now, just in case we forgot the rules of the pool, that even they never followed, they were kind enough to go over them again with us.

"No Band-Aids, no running on the deck, no underwear to be worn under the swim suits, and no food or gum in the pool area." The head lifeguard seemed to be important to me at the time. "Is there anything I am forgetting?" He looked at his fellow lifeguards for a response.

"Same shit as last year," Cesar said to me so the lifeguards couldn't hear. "They treat us like *we* are the campers." It was comforting to know he was willing to talk to me even though we had never met. Camp, the social lubricant. Just as strong as alcohol but without the hangover.

A short, round female lifeguard stood up and said, "All of you counselors must also be in the water or standing on the side of the pool in your swimsuits while the group is in the water." *Counselors?* Counselors in the Chicago Park District program were basically campers with hormones. Their only job was to help the recreation leaders, but instead they spent most of their time flirting. I remember being a counselor, but I certainly wasn't one anymore.

"Oh yeah, there can be too many kids for us to watch at times, so everyone needs to help," the head lifeguard added. Apparently we had to do their jobs for them. Maybe all the Big Macs were blocking memories of their extensive training program. Perhaps they simply did not like kids. Either way, I didn't understand how we had to help them do their job but they weren't expected to run a game of kickball or conduct arts and crafts with our kids. Eventually, I would begin to understand the truth that first summer.

Lifeguards and recreation leaders were very similar, *on paper*. We all worked with kids, were in the late teen to early twenties age group, and most importantly, we all loved our jobs. In reality, lifeguards are part of a fraternity of idiots who spend summer in an attempt to avoid work, get a tan, and get laid. Too bad our pool was inside.

When the lifeguards were finished, Julie guided us out of the pool area and on a quick tour of the rest of the building. We peeked into the auditorium and art room upstairs, and then back downstairs and into the gym. She instructed us to sit for a few minutes as she specified some more important rules: stay with your groups at all times, what to do if a camper gets hurt, and the steps to take in case you have to miss a day of camp. Then, she called us up to get our Chicago Park District Staff shirts. This was the equivalent of being knighted by the Prime Minister. When it was my turn, Julie tossed me two size large teal shirts. This made it official, I was a rec. leader. Once everyone had their shirts Julie called our attention for her final words. "There are only six weeks of camp each summer and they go by fast. Be prepared each day," she reminded us. "Now, fold up your chairs, go home, and I'll see you all on Monday."

Almost everyone was out the door in a flash. I was so happy just to be sitting in The Park's gym that I didn't care if I moved at all until Monday. *Could staying in one position for three days hurt?* I noticed I was the only one still sitting down, so I stood and started folding up my chair.

the hallway and I was free to browse my binder. I studied my group list in an attempt to become familiar with my campers' names. This was impossible; they all seemed to have the same name. Right on cue, James and Derek walked in together. James pulled up a seat next to me, and looked over our group's list as well. He pointed out which boys were in his group last year and if they were going to give us any sort of trouble. We had barely begun talking when Julie entered with the rest of the rec. leaders who must've been waiting out in the hall.

"Good morning everyone! What's going on? How are we today…excited? Good!" Her facial expressions and simple words relieved all of the tension that was going on in the pit of my stomach. I knew that if my boss was this relaxed then I should have nothing to worry about.

A quick ten-minute meeting in which Julie recapped some first day steps that we had discussed at our training and we were out the door and ready to meet our campers. Camp began at ten o'clock, but of course there were campers waiting to be greeted early at nine forty five. I followed Derek and James out the door and into the main hallway. We still had five minutes until we really had to be outside, so we grabbed tables and chairs and hauled them to our meeting area, by the field in back of the park house. These were the same spots I used to meet my rec. leaders every morning when I was a camper. It was nice to know that some things never change.

The female rec. leaders were also preparing for the first day and I was trying to put names to faces as I passed them in the hall. "Is that Jen?" I whispered to Derek as we made our second trip inside for another round of tables. I knew she worked last year, and was pretty sure of the name, and even some stories that went along with her, but wanted to double check.

Derek turned to see who I was looking at, "Yeah that's Jen alright. In about two minutes she will tackle James and well, violate him."

Right then James was making his way back inside as we were exiting. "Your girlfriend is looking for you," I said to him with a wink.

"Your mom is here?" he responded.

"Yeah she is, her and Jen are waiting to double team you," I responded seriously, looking up at the clock. *Almost time to meet the group.*

"Wouldn't be the first time," James said. "Besides, Jen is Derek's girl." He looked at Derek who darted outside shaking his head in disapproval.

"Explain," I said.

"Well, at the drive-in last year. Jen and Derek were on the roof of Becky's car making noises all night." Now he had my attention. "And all of a sudden Derek's belt comes off of the roof."

"It was a joke!" we hear coming from outside.

"So if anything, Derek is the one she wants," James said to me.

"Time to go," I reminded him nodding up to the clock on the hallway wall.

"I'll be right out," he said.

I walked down the back steps, passing Derek on the way. His group of younger boys met in the gym. "So you and Jen, I thought you liked Katie?"

"Hey, not so loud," he said. "I hope you know I wouldn't get with Jen."

"I know how desperate you are," I mocked him.

"Thanks man, you're a good friend."

"Just kidding," I said walking back down the steps. "Good luck today." I opened up the table where the group would line up, took off my backpack, found the binder inside, and set it on the table. I used some tape and hung a piece of paper marked 9 and 10 year old boys from the front. James jumped down the steps and jogged to the table empty handed. "Jen almost swallowed me whole," he said. Then he pointed across the field toward the playground. "Look, the first campers of the year."

I turned my head and eyed the kids, some walking with parents and others on their own, crossing the park towards us. While my nervousness crept back slightly, I tried not to let it show. I know I would have managed with a group on my own, but having James there, not only as a friend but as a returning rec. leader, made things all that easier.

"I'm not exactly sure how many of you were in camp last year, but this year things will be run a lot differently," I began explaining some of the ideas James and I had talked about over the last few days with the group. "Usually, each camp day is just like the one before it. Softball in the morning, then art, swimming, lunch, dodgeball, football, and then it is time to go home."

James continued my thought, "Vince and I are not going to play the same games everyday because we think that's boring. While you will sometimes be allowed to decide on what games to play, we want you to be patient with us because we think some games we can teach you will be very fun. For example, right now we are going to go into the gym and learn a new game. We need you to be quiet and listen so that we do not have to explain the directions a million times." James and I were off to a good start. "Okay, everyone get your bags and line up for gym."

With the ever-useful binder in my hand I followed the group into the gym at the end of the line. Pinball, as James would call it, was the game we were to learn. Even I had no idea how to play. James tried to explain it to me numerous times the night before but I guess I needed to see it to really grasp the concept.

The campers sat against the wall and James began explaining, "The game we are going to play is called pinball.

Basically, it's dodgeball meets basketball." A simultaneous explosion of excited talking broke out from the group. "It is called pinball because it is just like you are in a giant pinball machine," a smile crossed James face as he spoke the words. I couldn't blame him, the campers were hooked already. "There will be many different objectives in the game. You can hit each other to earn points, shoot the ball across the court and into garbage cans and the hoop, or knock over cones."

A short, skinny Puerto Rican boy in our group named Alex Colon raised his hand. "So we get to throw basketballs at each other!?" he asked.

James shook his head in disgrace. "Alex how do you say your last name?" James did not even respond to his smart-ass remark. "*CO-lin* like a butthole, or *Cologne* like the spray?"

"*Cologne,*" Alex replied.

"I'm just going to call you Butthole," said James. Only two hours into our first day and I knew that James had already ruined a kid's life.

"Okay, but I'm going to call you Hillbilly Jim," Butthole said.

"Deal."

During this discussion the rest of the group started to get anxious. A tall and extremely wide Polish boy raised his hand.

"John-Paul right?" I said.

"Um, yeah, everyone calls me J.P.," he said. "I don't understand how to play the game."

"We haven't explained it yet," I responded.

"Yeah, but I don't think I have ever played a game where you throw basketballs at each other," J.P. said without confidence.

James jumped into the conversation, "What did Vince and I just tell you? You do not throw basketballs at each other in this game. We will use volleyballs. And now we need you to be patient or we will end up sitting for the next hour instead of playing. Should I keep explaining so we can play?"

A collective "yes" rang out from the group.

"Okay, now listen up."

Five minutes later the teams were set, the garbage cans and cones were placed, and the balls were dropped. Fifty minutes of confusing and laughing bliss later and the twenty-six nine and ten year old boys, our three counselors, James, and myself, had become a united team. A team that was on its way to having the best summer possible, and one that I was very glad to be part of.

After pinball the kids grabbed boxed lunches and took them outside to eat, just like when I was in camp. When the food was finished we started up a game of football. From my past experiences, if the campers had to organize their own game their emotions would take over, and yelling and fighting would soon follow. Therefore, James and I were the captains and quarterbacks of each team.

Midway through our back and forth battle, one of the smaller boys, Connor, dropped an easy touchdown pass. I was shocked to hear the rest of my team yelling at him, basically telling him to rethink his life. This can be very traumatic for a nine year old to hear, even more so when you know it's the first day of camp and you'll have to spend the rest of your summer with these people. That's when Butthole opened his mouth.

"Hey man, don't worry about it. The best way to shut those guys up is to catch the ball next time," he said to Connor. "Besides, have you seen any of them do any better?"

I could not believe what I just heard. This ten-year-old boy, who already I had labeled as a smart mouth punk, was giving grown up advice to someone his own age. As much as I would have liked to be the one to offer such great advice, I think having it come from someone Connor's age made it even more important. Having someone stick up for him really made his day, or at least I know if I were his age it would have made mine.

Something else happened during that game that I had never considered in the year that I was hoping to get a job at The Park. With the game tied at five, the kids were getting competitive. Not just those I had decided were the good athletes, but everyone who was playing. They cared about insignificant camp sports just as much as I had five years before. The next team to score was going to win, and both teams had determined that team would be them. Even though James and I are very competitive as well, we knew that leaving the game in the hands of the campers was more important.

"Come on defense, all we have to do is stop them from scoring and we can get the ball back," James hollered as he pointed out players to guard. "You in the yellow shirt, get him. Tall kid, yeah you, guard the kid with the long hair." He was like a war general out there on the football field among those ten-year-old boys. It's okay, James never had any little brothers to boss around growing up.

Right before the snap, Butthole ran over to me, "Vince, if you throw me the ball we will win the game." He spoke to me not with cockiness but with confidence.

"If you're open," I told him. "Ready, set, hike!"

Five seconds later James was running in after me and my team had only one chance of scoring. I let the ball go and as soon as I threw it I knew I had gotten carried away. Even twelve-year-old boys could not catch the ball that I just threw. It was too fast, too high, and there were too many kids waiting for it to come down.

"No way," James uttered as the ball began its missile-like descent.

Butthole jumped over everyone, including two fourteen year old counselors, tipped the ball up to himself, and caught it with one hand, all while running at a speed that would carry him into the end zone for a game winning touchdown.

"Yeah Baby!" My voice rang out throughout the entire field.

"Was that Butthole?" James asked in amazement.
"I love that kid!" was my only reply.

July '01

As the heat picked up, the summer continued to be a blast. New games and activities kept things fresh, which helped us avoid the boring midsummer trend. By the end of the first week, instead of just hoping to get them to play one game, we had our campers requesting multiple games at once. Butthole became not only our favorite camper, but also a friend. His humor kept us laughing throughout the long heat of July and his athletic abilities kept his teams nearly undefeated.

A small group of employees decided to hang out at North Avenue Beach after camp on the third Tuesday of camp. It was the first time most of us would hang out without wearing our teal camp shirts. Cassie and Veronica met up with James, Derek, and me at The Park, and we headed off down Irving Park Road towards Lake Shore Drive. Everything felt different without campers being around, but I was warming to the idea of hanging with new people. Derek commented on how different the girls looked outside of camp and James and I agreed. Nice clothes and makeup can have a positive effect. In fact, it was the first time I had really thought about the female specimen in a sexual manner since I last saw Leslie at the end of the school year. We arrived at North Avenue but had to park two blocks west of the beach because the lot was full. The five of us walked towards the lake together, catching up on what seemed like seventeen years of friendship we missed out on.

When we reached the sand we talked with the beach house, a huge building in the shape of a boat, behind us. Bathrooms, restaurants, phones, and shops can all be found inside the massive boat building, so it was a good location to wait for Jen, BOK, and Becky, who would be meeting us soon.

"Where are they?" James asked. "What side of the boat are they meeting us on, port or starboard?"

"Sir? I just hope those three can find the boat in general." Derek had a point.

"Well what if we are on the wrong side of the boat?" James asked jokingly, as if he was in some sort of panic.

"Maybe you should check to see where the front of the boat is," Veronica suggested, "so you can see which side is starboard."

"Which side *is* starboard?" Cassie asked the group.

"I think it's the right side," James said uncertainly. "Yeah, right side."

"The right side when you're on the boat or the right side when you're looking at the boat?" I asked him. "Just like in baseball, a lot of people confuse left and right field because of their perspective."

"Hmm, I got nothing," James said. "I'll go check to see where the front of the boat is." He sprinted to the front of the boat. In the process he crossed a cement bike path and collided with someone. In a blur, James landed in the sand on the other side of the path as the clipped biker flipped over the front of his bike and landed violently on the pavement. James was okay, the biker that he hit, not so much. We were not exactly sure how to react so Derek and I slowly went over to the biker to check on him. I could now see that the victim was an athletic looking forty-something year old African American man. He had already stood up and was holding his chin with his right hand.

"Are you okay?" I asked him. He didn't look mad and I couldn't see any blood.

"Um, yeah, I'm okay I think," he answered as he picked up his bike with his left hand.

"Did I hit you?" he asked me.

I looked over to James who was now jogging up to us. "No you hit him," I said, pointing to James.

"I'm really sorry sir," James said in a hurry. "I didn't see you and I think you hit the back of my leg." At this point James seemed more scared for the man, than of him.

"It's okay." The injured biker was now attempting to fix his bike, which looked bent in a few spots. "Am I bleeding?" he asked, removing his hand from his chin. Blood rushed down his hand, and even in the darkening sky we could easily see the wide gash left under his jaw line.

"Yeah, you are," Cassie said grimacing and backing away. Blood dripped off of his hand and chin. "You should get that checked at the medical place over there." She pointed towards the front of the boat, and whether or not it was starboard or port didn't seem to matter anymore.

"I'm really sorry," James said, knowing there was really nothing else he could do. "Do you want me to help you over there?"

"No thanks," the biker said, now walking on the side of his bike as he pushed it along.

"I guess that could have been worse," Derek said.

"How?" Veronica noted. "James almost killed that guy." Jen, BOK, and Becky had just appeared in the parking lot near the incident.

"What happened here?" Becky asked.

"James just killed that guy over there walking by his bike," I said.

"How?" Jen said, worried about James and his well-being. I know he wasn't up to talking about it, but there was really no way around it so he explained the story again, starting with starboard.

When he finished there were sirens approaching in the background. "They are coming for you James," Cassie joked. James looked down Lake Shore Drive towards the noise.

"That man is dead and now you're going to jail," I tried to lighten the mood, unsuccessfully. An ambulance and police car were now visible on the Drive. "Wouldn't it be crazy if they were coming here?"

James was finishing his story when Derek nudged me in my side. I looked at him and he raised his head and eyebrows towards the street. I followed his directions and saw the emergency vehicles getting off the Drive and turning towards the beach. "I think they are coming here," Derek said. We watched the vehicles drive right up to the giant boat structure and park in front of the medical station where our biker victim was now located. "We should go."

"They're not going to arrest James or anything," Veronica said. "We might be able to help."

"It's your choice James," Derek said, looking at him with complete seriousness.

He didn't even think it over. "Let's get out of here," he said, ending our evening.

The next day camp had a little different feel to it and soon the whole staff knew. We mostly tried to laugh off the situation, for James's sake, but someone had programmed our electronic sign, which was displayed over the office door, to read "Congrats to James, the starboard biker killer." Julie quickly put an end to that message when the campers started asking about it. She said something about parents, unnecessary, and lawsuit.

Just when we were forgetting about the incident, the lifeguards informed us of some unfortunate news. Because our lifeguards at Independence were not exposed to the sun all day, they seemed to be gaining intelligence and finding new ways to ruin our fun. As I passed by Becky to get a basketball from the gym I thought I heard her mumble.

"What?" I asked Becky as I slammed on the brakes.

"The pool is closed for the rest of the day," she reiterated.

"How come?"

"I am not sure, Julie just told me that."

"Great," my sarcastic response was heartfelt by Becky. I was not sure what to tell the group considering every five minutes they would ask, "When do we go swimming?" I decided that I would have Julie break the bad news to them herself, considering she was the one who made the call. I found her leaving the office.

"What's up with the pool situation?" I asked.

"Nothing, your group can go swimming now." She started pinning up some flyers on the bulletin board in the hall.

"Becky told me the pool is closed."

"Well, it was but the lifeguards said it is okay to swim in now. They had to clean it out."

"What was in it?"

"Um. I'll let them tell you."

"Okay, well then I guess my kids won't be killing me after all."

After a quick change in the locker room, the group was in the pool, including James and me. Our pool was not the best in the world, but having one inside was a big advantage against possible weather conditions. I had just resurfaced after a cannonball in the deep end when I decided to ask one of the lifeguards about the temporary pool closing. "So what was in the pool that had to be cleaned?"

She said back to me nonchalantly, "One of the kids went diarrhea in it, so we had to clean it."

I knew I had heard wrong. "Is that a joke?"

"No." She was not very keen on explaining and began walking towards the shallow end.

I yelled over the screams of my boys, "When did this happen!?"

"About thirty minutes ago," she said.

"Wait," I was dumfounded, "A kid pooped in the pool and you completely cleaned it out in thirty minutes?"

"Yeah."

"How is that possible?"

"You see that," she pointed over to the wall, "it's called a net. I scooped it out."

"And you just threw it all away? Weren't there, you know, chunks that you missed? It's like liquid"

"Well it was diarrhea, so really I don't think I got it all." All that was missing was the "Duh" at the end.

"What! Shouldn't you close down the pool for a while? Empty it out or something?"

James was on his way over to join the conversation. I think he overheard some of it and now was eager to find out if he was indeed swallowing poop water for the last ten minutes.

"We never empty the pool when this happens. We just -"

"How often does it happen!?" James interrupted.

"Well...once last week, but not for a while before that."

"Last week!" Now James was furious. "How come no one told us!"

"I don't know, some of the other rec. leaders knew."

"Great, I need to go shower," was the last thing I said that year to any of the lifeguards. I felt bad knowing what was in the pool, but I was not sure if I should tell my campers. The last thing I wanted was twenty-five angry parents yelling at me, looking for an explanation for the pools sudden closing. The lifeguards had used their power to keep us rec. leaders from knowing about the true contents of the pool water. It wasn't even as if they felt bad about everyone swimming in feces. No apologies were given, no explanations spoken. Shortly after the news broke I saw Derek, "Did you hear about the pool?"

"Yeah, those bitches."

"That's fucked up. The lifeguards should shut down the pool when that happens."

"You're preaching to the choir, sir."

"I hate the lifeguards."

"I concur."

It was Monday of the fourth week of camp and I was walking down my front steps. It was a great day. The middle of July can be brutal. Not today. The sun was warm but blocked by a cloud formation. Eight-five degrees with a nice breeze, perfect summer weather for Chicago.

I no longer needed a backpack because I was never swimming again. My towel and trunks were left at home. All I carried was my homemade lunch of a peanut butter and jelly sandwich, an orange, and a water bottle. I was walking with new confidence. Camp was half way over and I had survived. Working with kids can be stressful. It is a constant struggle keeping every camper happy, fed, and alive. I walked up the steps off of Springfield Avenue and into the main hallway, our new designated meeting area. I put my lunch in the office fridge and sat down on the steps next to Cesar.

He was talking to Cassie and Veronica and I joined them. I was glad I could hold a conversation with people I met just three weeks prior. In school I would go the entire year without feeling comfortable saying one word to some of my classmates. I wasn't sure why I was suddenly Mr. Social but I liked the new me. Plus, Cassie and Veronica were my age and that gave us a reason to stick together.

After hearing a few childhood stories about the girls, James walked in and was looking around terrified. The Jen attacks had gotten much worse and he was on the look out. "Have you seen her?" he asked me quietly, as though not to wake the sleeping beast.

"No, not yet," I told him. James pulled himself up and sat on the information counter, opposite the staircase I was sitting on. This counter, which was positioned in front of the staircase that went up to the girl's bathroom and gym balcony, was used more as a hangout area than the receptionist desk it was intended to be. The electronic ticket hung above, reminding parents to pack sunscreen for their kids.

"What are you two talking about?" Cesar asked, putting a temporary halt on his conversation with the girls.

"You don't see it every morning?" James asked Cesar before looking over to the door at Derek, who was just entering. Then he got an idea. "This is what she does." James halfway stood up on the counter and jumped down on unsuspecting Derek, who could only manage the words "Dear God Sir!" They somehow did not fall over so James wrapped his legs around him and began imitating Jen. "Oh James! Good Morning!" He cups his hands under his imaginary large breasts. "Are you hungry this morning!" Derek, laughing out of humor and fear, was fighting James off to no avail. James began humping Derek and making animal sex noises that sounded like monkeys at the zoo. "I'm soooooo glad you could make it this morning!" Then they fell. Derek would have not been happy if he was in a bad mood, but it was a camp morning and they laid on the ground full of laughter.

Cassie and Veronica were laughing in that timid way you do when someone makes a racist joke. Cesar sat dumbfounded. "Who are you talking about?" he asked anyone who would listen.

"Sir?" James said as he helped Derek off the ground.

"I'm guessing Jen," Cesar said.

"Yeah, every morning is like that."

"I think it's so cute," Veronica voiced her opinion. "She wants you James and you should give her a chance."

James gave her a look that would have made most five year olds cry. "Thanks Veronica, that really makes things better."

Gene dropped in that morning to let us know that we had done a great job at camp so far and to keep it up for the last three weeks. James, who was terrified of Gene and his near three hundred pound frame, made frightened gestures the entire talk. Mostly, he was relieved that Jen walked in during Gene's talk and he was safe from her morning groping.

Outside it was sidewalk chalk day, and James and I spent our morning censoring what our boys were writing. "Carlos, you can't write that!" I said assertively.

Carlos was the brother of rec. leader Cristina, which he took as a "get out of jail free" card. He looked up at me, surprised I was keeping an eye on his art. "I didn't write that," he said, "it was already there."

I looked at him and then back at his illustration, a fat man resembling Gene squatting over and shitting blue chalk. Michelangelo would be so proud.

"Okay," I was compromising with him, "can you wash it off for me then?"

"Yeah," he said proudly. He got up and headed for the water fountain. I called James over to show him the work.

He walked around me to get a better view of the shitting man. "Not bad," he said. "I just changed the word 'suck' into 'sock.' Who did this one?"

"Carlos, but he denies it," I told him.

James turned around. I thought he was looking for Carlos to yell at him. "Butthole! Get over here!" he screamed.

Butthole looked up with a hint of fear in his eyes. He slowly moved from his artwork and came over towards the two of us. "Did you call me?" his raspy voice had a hint of fear in it.

"Why did you draw this?" James asked him. "Some little girl came over here, saw it, and now she's crying." He was trying to hold a serious face.

"What are you talking about man?" Butthole questioned. "I didn't draw anything." He looked at the image I was now pointing at and began to laugh hysterically, "That's a good one!"

"It's not funny," James said angrily. "Gene saw it and now he wants whoever wrote it to go to his office. You're going to get kicked out of camp."

"James man, I swear I didn't draw that. Come on look at that, that shit is blue. I would never draw shit blue." Butthole was trying to make the situation funny. "And man that guy looks constipated."

"Everyone told me that you drew it," I said, teaming up against him. "We're sick of you lying to us."

"Vince man I'm not lying," he said, starting to get nervous. I looked up at James and could see him laughing. Butthole noticed also. "Hey, what you doing man? Are you guys messing with me?"

"We know it wasn't you," James said. "But if we see you writing anything inappropriate, you will be kicked out of camp."

Butthole was half mad half confused. He gave us one of those mean mobster looks and walked back over to where he was sitting. It was great to know that he understood the humor behind it. We didn't want a call from some pissed off parent. That would happen a week later.

Cesar, James, and I brought the nine, ten, and eleven year old boys down into the basement after lunch. No one ever went down into the basement, not even when I was a camper, but we gave out too many second chances and now it was time for consequences. The kids sat down in chairs filling in the dark, rectangular room. Cesar, James, and I stood. I began the talk.

"We are so tired of you guys not listening to us. We are not going to pick up after you when you eat anymore, like your little mommies or daddies do at home. It has come to a point where I would rather take the ten or fifteen good kids out of the forty of you and play football with them. We're tired of getting yelled at by our bosses for your messes." I was running out of things to say so I waved James into the ring. Tag Team.

"*I* want to talk about the talent show." James said. He waited a few seconds, gathering his thoughts. The kids were completely alert. "I don't like wasting an hour everyday practicing. It should take twenty minutes. I don't like making the kids who are paying attention suffer because some of you don't care."

Someone from the back of the room yelled "Yeah!"

"You think this is funny Carlos?" Cesar said.

"It wasn't me," Carlos replied.

"I saw you say it," Cesar said shaking his head in disgust. "Why would you lie about that? Most of you lie to us all the time too. We are trying to help you guys out, make this summer fun. But you guys all want to piss us off and make things hard on yourselves."

I just remembered a strategy Julie had taught us. I rattled off ten names and told those kids to stand up. I looked over at my counselor Joe Voigt. "Take these guys into the locker room with you to change. One of us will be up in a couple minutes." The room grew quiet as the group of well-behaved boys made their way upstairs to change for swimming. "Now," I began again, "if we can sit here quietly we will join them for swimming. Two minutes of no talking."

I looked over at James and Cesar, proud of the way we had finally stepped up to our campers and showed them we were not going to be pushed around anymore. The breaking point was twenty minutes ago, during lunch. Some of Cesar's boys, who spend a few hours a day with us, started playing baseball with oranges. Our boys followed along. In five minutes their game turned our entire eating area into an orange cemetery. Busted Tropicana's were spread out like body parts after Normandy. When time came to clean up the mess, the boys all played stupid, acting like they were not involved. Cesar, James, and I knew we weren't going to be the ones picking up the mess so we told them that if they didn't clean it up in two minutes, we were having a long talk in the basement. Apparently we weren't very threatening.

"One minute left," Cesar said. The room was still quiet and I assumed we had gotten through to them. Then I heard talking.

"Looks like we are starting over," I said to the room. "Some people don't know how to keep their mouth's closed." The countdown started over at two minutes. Thirty seconds later it started over again. And again. And again. Finally we decided to let the campers who were quiet upstairs to swim. Cesar accompanied them. About fifteen campers remained, mostly from mine and James's group.

J.P. was raising his hand. I did not want to do him any favors but he looked concerned. "Yes John Paul?"

"I have to go to the bathroom," he said. An old, dark bathroom was in the room next to us.

"There is one right here. Hurry up."

"I have to take a crap," he explained. Most of the kids started laughing. James did too.

"Well you better check to see if there's toilet paper," I warned him trying not to laugh myself.

He shuffled into the bathroom, over to the stall, and looked inside. He must have seen toilet paper because he closed the door. The room erupted with laughter.

"Two minutes!" James said.

"The next person that talks is going to sit in the bathroom," I said. The ultimate punishment.

"Man, J.P. is going to stink up the whole basement," Carlos said. Ten seconds later he was sitting outside of J.P.'s stall.

James and I spent twenty more minutes in the basement. James moved some kids to the corner of the room. I tried to make kids work for their freedom. "Ten pushups and you can go swimming," I said to Carlos. I knew he was too big to even do two.

"If I do ten can I go upstairs?" Butthole asked.

"If you can write me a letter of apology you can go upstairs," I countered.

"Forget that," he said sitting back down. "There's shit in that water anyway." Word traveled fast at Independence.

Some of the kids started to complain. They were unwilling to formally apologize with a letter or complete the "challenges" I asked them to do. In the end we missed all of swim time and cleaned up the park for the rest of the day.

The next day *I* was the one sitting in Gene's office. "So Mr. Tipre, I have gotten three phone calls from parents complaining about some incident yesterday in the basement." For the first time in my life Gene was pissed at me. "What the hell happened?"

I explained to him how we brought them downstairs to talk to them about their behavior and how we let those who were behaving leave to swim.

"I heard you made them do pushups," Gene said. "Please tell me that didn't happen."

I was fucked. Game over. Fired in my first year. If I was going down I was at least going to show Gene the respect he deserved. I lied. "What? No. I told them that 'if anyone can do ten pushups then you can go swimming.' I didn't *make* anyone do anything." I thought of Carlos in the bathroom with J.P.'s smell. I hope his mom didn't complain.

"Okay, but I have to write you up at least. One more incident and I'll have to fire you, Mr. Tipre." I usually liked when he called me by my last name. It made me feel important, like we were old pals. Not now.

"I'm sorry, Gene." I left his office with my job but without my dignity. *At least I know I can never do that again.*

That night I went home and thought about what I was doing wrong as a rec. leader. I had copied the actions of my rec. leaders growing up without realizing that things had changed. I yelled at my campers and lacked techniques to control them and myself. I decided that I would have to try and make some changes in the future if I wanted to keep my sanity and my job.

August '01

Derek worked with the six year old boys that summer, and while I first assumed that that meant James and I would not be able to hang out with him much, I soon realized that camp was basically a six week long party. All of the rec. leaders talked before, during, and after camp everyday, until the point where people I had never even met six weeks ago were some of my best friends.

The end of camp always meant two things: the talent show for the campers and evaluations for the rec. leaders. I did not know what to expect when Julie called me into her office in the middle of the final soccer game of the year.

"First things first, are you coming back next year?" I was not sure if Julie was asking out of her own curiosity or if that was one of the questions on the form. I tried to glance at what she was writing but felt that she would notice. "I just need you to sign at the bottom," she said after a few seconds.

"Okay," I said, taking the evaluation from her. I looked at the markings on top. Check marks filled the "meets expecta-tions" middle column. While there were no checks in the "needs improvement" column; the "exceeds expectations" section was also blank. I wasn't sure if this was good or bad.

"I give everyone 'meets expectations,'" she said. "So no one feels better or worse than anyone else. I think it's fair."

"Yeah, that makes sense," I said. I signed and handed her back the paper. "Is that it?"

"Yep, that's it." I got up and headed for the office door. Then she asked again, "Are you coming back next year?"

"Are you kidding? I'm working here until I die!" I told her with a smile on my face.

I soon found out that Julie was not the only one who wanted to know if I was coming back next year. It seemed everyone became hooked on the future and forgot about the present. I decided that I would wait until next year to try out new disciplinary techniques. The yelling was holding me over for now. The last week of camp had become centered on the phenomenon of "next year." Kids ran wild as Becky and James discussed next year's field trips. The movies and museums would remain, but the beach and zoo needed to be axed, they decided. Veronica and Cassie were always commenting on how next year would never come for them. They had been ready to quit after two weeks.

"Next year I will probably be working at Hooters," Veronica said honestly. "Anything is better than this job."

"There is no job better than this," I corrected her. "You get paid to hang out with me all day."

"Exactly, worst job of all time."

"Wow, thanks."

During this time it was not uncommon to find Cesar hanging out with our coworker, Cristina, in the auditorium as his group played soccer in the field. Just as it was likely Joe Voigt would be off with counselor Caitlin right when I needed someone to take a bleeding camper to the office. Sometimes the last week was so out of control that rec. leaders lost their entire groups.

"Do you know where my group is?" Derek said to me aimlessly later that day. "They were by the playground a second ago."

I was in the middle of a conversation with Butthole so it took me a second to comprehend. "Sir? You have been playing softball with James for the last half hour," I reminded him. "Besides, how can your whole group be gone? Where are they supposed to be?"

"IN THE PLAYGROUND VINCE!" he yelled.

I countered with, "I don't know why you're mad at me, I didn't lose your campers."

"This is not funny," he said running towards field house.

"It's a little funny," Butthole said back.

"Be careful," I yelled after him. "Julie might find out before your evaluation!"

James had a smirk on his face as he jogged over to me. "He still doesn't know where they are?"

"He has no idea," I said. "But he's mad."

James looked confused, "Why would he be mad? He lost the group. Julie's the one who should be mad. He's lucky all she did was move his group into the Women's Building. She could have fired him."

"There he goes again," Butthole said pointing towards Derek.

We turned to see Derek running across the field towards the Women's Building. "Maybe Julie told him," I guessed. "She must have felt bad."

"Now Derek is going to blame me," James said. "'If you hadn't called me over to play softball, then she wouldn't have taken my group,'" James's impersonation of Derek was perfect.

Even I became obsessed with next year. I wanted a complete list of all returning rec. leaders so I knew who to keep in contact with over the winter. Even though I was now close with most of the employees, there was no need to talk to people I would probably never see again. Also, I wanted to see if there would be open positions for next summer. Nick was sick of hearing park stories for another summer and became interested in joining us next year. So, I wanted to present the idea to Julie as soon as I could.

With two hours left on Friday, camp was coming to an end. For the first time in my life I allowed myself to become part of a new social group. I went to parties at foreign houses and spent time with unfamiliar people. I sat on the pool deck while my campers were swimming, thinking about the up coming school year. I decided that my new friends would help balance out my typical routine. One night homework, one night basketball with Nick, one night partying with the rec. leaders. I liked it.

Hanging out with this new group of people had many benefits. Aside from never being bored at night or on the weekends, the female rec. leaders were cute. They were part of the new me. Girls that I could talk to for hours upon hours about random camper stories or late night memories from that first summer. With my summer friends around, the world of high school, including Leslie, was far from my thoughts.

In general, thinking negatively about anyone from The Park would be very hard to do. I figured that the upcoming school year would mean a fresh approach to high school for me. I was going to take the new experiences from over the summer and use them to relax more during my senior year, have more fun, meet new people, and most importantly, get into a good college. If camp was this much fun, I could not imagine how great college must be.

Two hours later I had said goodbye to all of my campers, save one. Butthole was going to hang out with James and I at my house after camp. Derek was weirded out by the situation and he was not the biggest fan of Butthole, who would repeatedly joke around with him about his hairy chest. Just last week, at our field trip to River Park's Olympic size outdoor pool, Butthole told Derek that he would never get a girlfriend until he shaved that "thing" growing on his chest. He was not amused.

James, Butthole, and I walked into my house and set down our belongings behind my front door. Butthole was looking around as if my house was a museum. He pointed to a doll my mom had set on the entry table, "Hey man, is that Harriet Tubman?" James and I looked at his honest facial expression, then the doll he was pointing at. I almost died when I saw the truth behind his words. I was struggling to catch my breath in between laughs, "No, that's just a doll my mom bought from an antique store." I picked up the doll and showed James. It did look like Tubman, or at least as much as I knew from pictures I saw in history books.

James took the doll from me, "How do you even know who Harriet Tubman is?"

"Who me?" Butthole asked.

"Yeah."

"I read about her in social studies," Butthole said. "I saw a picture of her freeing the slaves and it looked just like that. She was wearing the same dress too."

"That's awesome," James said. He put the doll back on the table. "Hey man, is that Harriet Tubman?" he said imitating Butthole.

"I thought it was," Butthole said, following me and James to the couch. "Are we going to order pizza or what? My mom said I have to be home at five."

"Yeah, I'll order it." It was pretty cool that his mom trusted us enough to let him hang out. Or, perhaps he never really told her where he was at. I grabbed the phone and called La Villa. As it rang I watched James and Butthole talk about the White Sox and how they needed to pick up the pace if they intended on making the playoffs. Then it finally hit me: camp was over, what remained of summer would soon follow, and senior year would be arriving soon. I forced myself to hold on to that day as long as I could.

Year Two

April '02

Senior year was one long going away party. Long would be an exaggeration however, because it felt like one day I was dreading my first day back at school for my final year and the next I was preparing for prom. If *Blitzkrieg* meant "lightning war," then the twelfth grade was *Blitzyear*.

Fall semester was filled with memories of driving to school everyday, now that my dad had granted me temporary custody over the Mystique. Keith, a good friend from Lane, would get dropped off at my house every morning. We would drag our tired bodies into the car before we scooped up Derek, Dale, and Sean. Dale was now a freshman at Lane, and because we went to the same school and knew some of the same people, the gap in our ages seemed almost gone. Sean, another Lane friend who, like me, was hoping on attending U of I. Talks of possibly rooming together made the morning drive something to look forward to.

"I can't wait," he said one morning. "Playing Halo and eating pizza all night."

"That's what we do now," I reminded him.

"I know, it's going to be amazing!"

"I've got my fingers crossed."

The pressure of senior year was over by the time April came around because college acceptances letters were already received, fates already sealed. Fortunately, Sean and I were both accepted into the U of I at the Urbana-Champaign campus downstate, where we would soon be roommates. Derek had decided not to stay in Chicago, opting to apply to the west coast at the University of Arizona instead. I secretly hoped he wouldn't get in, but around spring break he received his acceptance letter in the mail. Despite Derek's eventual departure, knowing that I was going to be attending my college of choice, a top academic and party school, boosted my confidence in my final year of high school. Confidence that could cure me of my Leslie tunnel vision.

So, naturally, I spent most of senior year chasing Leslie around the halls of my high school hoping for her to break up with her boyfriend and marry me. At times, I did have Cassie and Veronica around to distract me. I continued talking to them during the school year and became close to Cassie in particular. She told me she wanted to go on a few dates and see what happened, but every time I was thinking about pulling the trigger and making it official, Leslie would come around and screw up everything. I was no longer free and confident. I lost track of everything I had learned during my first summer at The Park, such as allowing myself to branch out and try new things. For months I constantly persuaded Leslie to sign up to work at The Park for the upcoming summer, but to no avail. So, when she actually went over spring break and filled out an application, I was overjoyed. Nick, not needing my persuasion, also applied for one of the positions left vacant by a non-returning rec. leader.

Camp had held such a special place in my heart for so many years, and now I hoped it would take on an even greater meaning. My first year working at The Park was a time to jump into the flow of things. I turned seventeen that summer and was the youngest employee. Many of the other rec. leaders were in their twenties and had seniority over me, so I pretty much laid back and tagged along. There were several traditions already in place, the drive-in movies, the beach, and the end of the year party to name a few, but they felt like they belonged to the older crowd. When my first summer ended and three of the older workers decided that they were not going to be returning, I took that as a chance to make The Park my place. I was already close with most of the rec. leaders and my house across the street was the typical hangout. I felt like the center of it all, and helping Leslie and Nick get hired was my way of staking claim to the day camp way of life.

June '02

Graduation came a few days before camp started and I spent that evening celebrating with my closest Lane friends. The girl I was seeing at the time, Jerilyn, drove over to my house with Megan, whom Derek and I spent the last four years together with in homeroom. Finally now, at the end of senior year, Megan and I were becoming close friends. The three of us met with Nick, Sean, Derek, Keith and another friend Edgar, at the Steak N' Shake by the Allstate Arena, where we reminisced about the last four years as we ate chicken fingers and burgers. Edgar recently signed the paperwork to join me and Sean as roommates at U of I, and the group joked about daily fights we were going to have.

"Edgar isn't going to let anyone in his car with him and you two will have to walk to get groceries," Megan said, pointing out Edgar's passion for his black Mustang.

"Hell yeah," Edgar said, "you bitches are walking!"

"Edgar, you're so gay," Keith slid in a comment.

"Sir, have you seen yourself?" Edgar asked with his entire hand pointing towards Keith. "You are famous around school for always taking your clothes off."

"Edgar, you get me so mad!"

"And they're off," Jerilyn said. The waiters knew us pretty well and didn't seem to mind the commotion being that it was midnight and the place was empty. We watched the two of them spar with each other for the third time that day. Edgar would talk shit, sneak in for a cheap shot, and run for his life when Keith decided it was time to return the favor. They thought it was their own little fight club.

We finished our food and I couldn't help but feel everything must be a dream. High school was over and I had two months of freedom ahead of me. We parted ways, except for Jerilyn, who came to my house to get her car. I asked her to walk across the street to The Park and she said she would. We sat on the bench on the small hill across the field from the park house. I was debating how to tell Jerilyn what was on my mind, but I knew that it had to be done.

"I have to tell you something," I started. She looked at me and I continued. "Last summer was the best of my life. I was single, and even though I didn't even hook up with anyone, it felt good being able to do whatever I wanted." Her face was surprisingly calm. "I think we have some great times together…but I just can't be exclusive with you during the summer."

She looked away towards the playground and I hoped she wasn't crying. "Is it because of Leslie working here this summer?" she asked bluntly, still looking away.

"Yes, that's a part of it." Honesty is the best policy. "I have liked her for so long and I don't think I could forgive myself if I didn't use this summer as my last effort to find out if she feels the same."

Jerilyn turned back to me, without tears in her eyes. That much was a relief. "Vince, it sucks, but it's okay. I want to be able to be off with my friends and not have to worry about you or have you worry about me either. I mean, this is our last summer before college, and if we are dating, then we won't have time for everyone else."

"Yeah, I know. Plus we're going to school together in the fall. The Leslie thing will probably blow up in my face anyway and I'll end up apologizing to you for ever even wanting this."

She smiled at me and stood from the bench. "I'm going to go home and get some sleep. Walk me to my car."

"Okay," I said. "Can we get some park water on the way?"

"Sure Vince," she said. "You and your park."

I liked the sound of that.

Right before camp started I spent my final days working at my family's hardware store. I told my dad that I really wanted to concentrate on camp and then even get a job working with kids year round.

I remember introducing our two newest co-workers to the rest of the rec. leaders when training arrived. Nick was already friends with James and Derek, but seeing him comfortable with everyone else was encouraging. Leslie, on the other hand, was just as she had always been, friendly but distant. Cesar tried to make Leslie feel like part of the group, but even his help was insufficient. It appeared she was going to have an interesting summer fitting into the day camp way of life, not only as a rec. leader, but as a friend. While her clinging to me during the annual pool tutorial boosted my ego, I could already tell that having her around was going to complicate the simple life that camp usually hosted. Even the counselors had mixed signals from Leslie. Joe Voigt, who was now almost to the age where he could become a rec. leader, loved the idea of having an attractive new female in the mix. Caitlin, who was the same age as Joe Voigt, showed me right off the bat that having Leslie around was not pleasing everyone.

"So, who is that new girl?" Caitlin said snobbishly, and I immediately wondered if the rumors of her crush on me last summer were true.

"Oh, just a friend of mine from school."

"She looks like a bitch." Caitlin also liked Leslie.

"She's nice, once you get to know her." With that Caitlin walked away towards Joe Voigt. Both of them, like Dale, just finished their freshman year at Lane. Seeing them in the halls was like seeing a teacher at the grocery store, you have no reason to think they shouldn't be there, but the sight still makes your head hurt. In short, I was starting to realize that these counselors, while working under me, were going to be rec. leaders themselves in a year or two.

When the time came to get placed into groups, Julie split up me and James. He would stay with the younger boys from last year and Cesar and I, with Joe Voigt as our counselor, would take over the oldest boy group. I felt that working with Cesar was not going to be as fun and was hesitant towards managing the group with him. We sat down and started sorting through emergency forms and paperwork, sending Joe Voigt on various busywork tasks in the meantime. I immediately searched for Butthole's name and even had to catch myself flipping through the 'Bs.' I was relieved when I found his registration form and temporarily stopped and wondered if everyone at camp was still going to call him Butthole this summer. My decision was cut short as Cassie approached our table with one of the new rec. leaders at her side.

"I just wanted to let you know that this is Ashley," she said. "She is my cousin."

Cesar and I looked up to acknowledge the new member of our team. "Hey," Cesar said, "what group are you going to be with?"

"Julie has me with play camp," Ashley responded.

"Sorry," I consoled her.

"Actually I wanted the young kids, so I'm pretty happy right now." I looked from Ashley to Cassie, who was eyeing Leslie. I wondered if she knew that Leslie was the reason I swayed away from dating her.

"Is that your friend?" Cassie asked me, still looking at Leslie. "How come she is sitting by herself?"

"Yeah, Leslie. She's a good friend from school." I informed her. "I don't know why she's sitting alone though.

You two should go talk to her." Unlike Nick, who was completely self sufficient, I felt that if I didn't force the issue, Leslie would spend the summer as a ghost.

"Maybe later," Cassie said. She looked at Ashley who exchanged a look of pity. "Well, I can tell this is going to be a fun summer."

"Nice meeting you Ashley," I said to her as they began to walk back to their table.

"You too Vince."

I watched the girls walk away and saw another face I didn't recognize, a tall, pale looking white guy. I figured I should introduce myself now, rather than later, because six weeks of camp could come and go in a flash and I wanted to maximize the time I had. I told him my name and he said his was Mike. "So which one of these girls do you have your eye on Vinny?" he asked casually.

"Ha, well...the one alone at the table over there," I motioned towards Leslie. "She's a friend from high school and I have had my eye on her for a long time now."

"You mean the bitch looking girl?"

"That's the one."

"She is smoking though."

"Haha, thanks."

"Hey Vince, come here a sec," I heard Cesar's voice from a few tables over.

"Okay Mike, well I need to get back to my stuff. Welcome to the team."

"Thanks Vinny."

After a tour of the remodeled basement and brief explanation of our responsibilities, it was time to hit the road. Training was over and Leslie still had not spoken a word to anyone. I knew then that summer number two was going to be much different.

"Where is your friend?" Our morning meeting in the new basement art room ended and already Gene was interrogating me.

"What friend?"

"Leslie, she's not here," Gene said, but I hadn't even noticed. "I swear I should just retire already and avoid all this crap."

"Oh, I'm not sure where she is. Should I call her?" I was beginning to feel like I made a big mistake asking Gene and Julie to hire her.

"No, I'll call her," Gene ended the conversation as he walked towards the office to use the phone. I only hoped Leslie would walk through the front door in the next ten seconds so I would not have to worry anymore.

"Twenty minutes late on her first day. I told you she was a bitch," a voice said behind me.

"Good morning to you too Caitlin. What group are you with this year?"

"Cristina's, as usual. Well, have fun."

"Haha, very funny." It was fine with me if people didn't like Leslie. She was not working at The Park to be everyone's friend; she was there to fall in love with me.

Julie came out of the office, "Jennifer, you have to take on the seven year old girls by yourself today." Before she even finished her sentence I knew what that meant.

"Is Leslie not coming?" Jen replied.

"Nope."

"Are you serious?" I questioned. "Is she sick?" I could not believe she took off her first day.

"No, apparently she will be out of town today and tomorrow." Julie's answer did not make any sense.

"Out of town? Where the hell is she?"

"Mexico."

"Mexico? And she didn't tell you or Gene this at training?"

"Not a word about it."

"Fire her ass." I meant it.

"If she does not show up on time on Wednesday, I will. Now, go outside and wait for your kids." Julie ended that meeting in a heartbeat.

As the kids arrived I cheered up when I realized a camper from last year, Gabe, was in James's group. That kid would show off his smart-ass mouth to anyone who would listen, and now I would be able to laugh at the humor without being accountable for the fallout that ensued.

A few minutes later I found out that camp was more important to the kids than I originally thought. While they lined up by groups, most of them began talking and reminiscing about last summer. Butthole showed up ten minutes late and I was surprised by how similar he looked from last summer. My question on what to call him was answered before he even signed in, as cries of "Butthole!" rang throughout The Park.

"I missed you Vince," were Butthole's first words to me.

"I missed you too, Butthole. I'm glad you are back."

"Me too Vince, me too."

After a few morning name games we ate lunch. This time was spent explaining Leslie's whereabouts to Katie, James, and Derek. They had some input on the situation but we quickly transitioned to joking about the always-great names some of the kids have.

"Sasquel Exum," Derek said. "Now that name sounds like a super hero or something."

"Yeah it does." James said.

"Well, I know a kid named Nosmo King," Katie seemed eager to share this information. "He was a student in a classroom I observed for school."

"He ruled Egypt during the third century I believe," Derek the history buff chimed in.

"Wait, wait, wait. I asked him where he got that name, and he said his mom couldn't think of anything so, she named him after the first name she saw after she gave birth," Katie had now drawn the interest of Cesar and Joe Voigt as well. "Nosmo King, get it?"

"No," Cesar answered.

"His mom named him after the No Smoking sign!"

"WHAT! Bullshit," Cesar tried to talk over the laughter of the rest of us.

"I swear," Katie said. She was too innocent to think she was lying. "I didn't think it was real, so I even asked his mom how he got his name. She told me the same story."

"And I thought the name Butthole was messed up," James was ready to roll over with laughter.

"That's great! Nosmo King!" Joe Voigt's words made us all think and appreciate, if only for a second, about how we were lucky to not be named "Stop," "Yield," or "Slippery Whenwet."

During lunch I was able to set aside my first day worries about Leslie and concentrate on what I loved about camp: Spending time with friends, playing games outside, and shaping the minds of twenty something kids on a daily basis. This year I welcomed back some of the same campers as last year. Julie setup camp this way so that each rec. leader would move up an age group to have the same campers as the previous year. I really appreciated this because I did not want to have to start over and learn the names, skills, and behaviors of a new set of kids. It took me three days my first year to learn all of the kids names but by the end of the first day the second time around, I could name everyone without hesitation.

When Leslie showed up on day three I was not that glad to see her. She did not seem to care that she missed days, let alone apologize to me for getting her the job and then making me look bad. Either way, with her at camp, the amount of drama tripled from year one.

Everyday felt like an episode of *One Life to Live*:

"Why don't you break up with your boyfriend and be with someone that cares for you?" Vince questions Leslie.

"It's not that easy." Leslie wipes a tear from her eye, "I love him."

"No one that loves you would treat you that way." Vince moves in next to Leslie and lifts her chin with his hand.

"So who should I be with?" Leslie seems to be asking with complete honesty even though it is completely obvious.

"Me."

"It would never work Vince. I do not want to ruin our friendship, it is too important to me."

"Okay," Vince seems hurt and confused but still replies, "how about if we just make out?"

Soap Operas may seem like a great stretch of reality, but Leslie played the lead role as if she had a script in hand. I was never sure if the rest of the rec. leaders hated Leslie and her constant complaining and crying over her boyfriend, hated me for getting her the job, or just did not care about the situation at all.

July '02

During week two I spilled my heart out to Leslie one last time, hoping she would realize how much she meant to me and how we needed to be together. I almost went as far as making a mix tape, but I knew it would just be a waste. She simply did not see me as anything more than a friend.

After my last attempt to be with Leslie failed, I finally made the steps needed to concentrate on other people out there. Two years of my life dedicated to trying to be the perfect guy for this one girl, and for nothing.

I also decided that I needed to make up lost time with my campers. Leslie had helped make my situation at The Park awkward, to say the least, but I intended to spend the rest of the summer fixing my mistakes. The first thing I did was treat my group to a day of dodgeball and pizza. My friends came next.

"Let's go out for your birthday," Mike suggested. As a new rec. leader this year, I figured Mike to be someone who did not want to socialize with the tight knit group we had become. I'm glad I was wrong.

"Sounds good, I need some time with the guys. What did you have in mind?" I asked.

"The strip club."

"Strip Club! When are we going?" James had not had a girlfriend in quite some time.

"Friday, for Vinny's eighteenth birthday."

"Don't mess around with me because I have always wanted to go," James's tone was surprisingly serious.

"I'm serious, Friday night," Mike responded promptly. I believed he was a strip club pro from the laxness of the discussion.

"Sounds good, I'll go tell everyone. What time?" I eagerly asked.

"I don't know, let's say nine."

"Okay." James and I walked back over to our groups. We would be eating for another ten minutes so we knew there would be time to talk to Derek, Nick, and Cesar about joining us.

"You have got to love that we can get paid to plan outings to strip clubs," James brought up.

"True, but it's not like our job wouldn't be great if we had to just play soccer and dodgeball all day like we are supposed to."

"This is the life."

"I concur."

Friday night was possibly the best night of my life. Nick couldn't come but my roommate Sean filled in nicely. James, Derek, Mike, Sean, and I piled into my red Mystique and off we went to the Admiral. From the conversation we were having when we arrived, they were committed to showing me a good time. Yes, seeing naked women dancing was a big part of that, but going out with the guys and not having to worry about Leslie anymore felt like a weight had been lifted. I was no longer going to worry about girls in the same manner. If a relationship happened then great, but spending countless hours trying to force one is a mistake I would never make again. Right now, I was only worried about the news I just received from the guys.

"At eleven they are going to put you on stage," the smirk on Mike's face worried me.

"What are you talking about?" I demanded an explanation that would end with "just kidding Vince."

"We got you a dance on stage with any two strippers that you want," Derek was not providing the words I needed to hear.

"Are you serious? Ummmm, who paid for this?" I looked around at everyone, hoping someone's face would tell me who was to blame. Sean was busy getting a lap dance from a stripper with massive breasts and James was busy staring at Sean getting a lap dance from a stripper with massive breasts.

"We all did," Mike answered.

"Dear god sir. What strippers should I pick?"

"Whoever you want, this is your day man." While I knew Derek was being honest, I was scared to pick a girl that the guys thought was second rate.

"Okay, sign me up for Heaven and Kylie."

"Good picks," said Derek.

Nights like the strip club were very common during the six weeks of day camp. Aside from the naked women, dancing, and flying dollar bills, each night the rest of summer two was just as fun as that one. Katie, who was the oldest rec. leader out of the bunch, usually planned the wild outings for the rest of us. Even though she was going to be a senior in college, she still had the personality of a fifteen year old. Always ready to drink some beers, yell at old people, or tell a fart joke, Katie was the life of the party.

Halfway through camp the summer heat reached its peak. It was so bad that on Wednesday of the third week Nick had to leave work early from dizziness. The timing could not have been worse. I had decided to take advantage of the offer my uncle made me to have some people over at his house that night. He was out of town for a week and I assumed he and my aunt would not mind a small get together. I knew Nick was bed ridden, but I was still somewhat mad he couldn't attend my first hosted party.

I decided to invite rec. leaders only. I just felt that my high school friends would feel out of place. Mostly, I did not want the party getting out of hand. There were twenty rec. leaders altogether and fifteen would show at most, by my calculations.

Fifteen turned into thirty very fast.

"Where should I put my beer?" asked Mike.

"In the fridge downstairs," I told him. "Just find a space next to the other liquor. There may not be enough room so you might have to leave some on the floor for now."

"Sounds good Vinny." I could hear Mike fumbling with the beer downstairs and I was tempted to help him out when I heard the doorbell ring. I yelled for Cesar to open it as Mike ascended from the basement. "Want a beer?" He had three cans of Bud Light in his hand.

"Thank you," I said.

"Let's get started." I opened my can and Mike opened the other two.

"Are you drinking both of those?"

"Of course Vinny."

"Two weeks ago I hadn't even talked to you and now you are my strip club buddy who is double fisting beers at my aunt's house."

"It takes a little while for me to settle in."

I mingled amongst my coworkers and met some of their uninvited friends until I got to Leslie and Cristina. Cristina was the only rec. leader Leslie really seemed to click with, and while I was done with Leslie and her bullshit, I was still intrigued when I heard she broke up with her boyfriend.

"He found out I'm here and he is trying to find out where this house is so he can come and get me," Leslie said.

"I'm just letting you know that if he comes here he is going to get his ass beat," said Cristina. I am sure Cristina was as sick as I was of hearing how he treats her like shit and is overly possessive. "Vince will beat his ass."

"Honestly, he better not come here Leslie. I won't let him in the house." I just wanted her to understand that I was clear in my opinion of her boyfriend.

"He is not coming over," said Leslie.

"Good, then everything will be fine." Before I walked away I said, "I hope you find someone that makes you feel happy because you deserve it." I said this in front of Cristina and some other guests as well, but I didn't care, I meant it.

Just as I was entering the kitchen I bumped into Caitlin coming up the basement stairs. "Oh, sorry Vince."

"It's okay." I noticed a couple of beers in her hands. "Aren't you a little too young to be drinking?"

"And you're not?" She had me there. "These are for Mike anyway. You know he has drunk like fifteen beers already?"

"That doesn't surprise me, he opened two as soon as he walked in the door."

"Yeah, I think he's funny." Caitlin pushed up against me as someone walked past us. I suddenly had the urge to kiss her. I stared at her longer than I should have. Her face was to die for. So was her underage body. Fuck. Game over.

"Caitlin, if only you were a little older," I said as a smile crossed my face.

"What?"

"I said, 'if only you were older.'"

"Yeah right," she was sure I was kidding.

I knew Caitlin had liked me for the better part of a year now and I really did think she was great, but she was a sophomore in high school and I was in college. "I'm serious. Someday Caitlin, seriously."

"You're drunk."

"Honestly I'm not." Actually I was, but I was not lying to her about the possibility of a future. She seemed to blush as she walked over to Mike, Katie, and Joe Voigt with a couple of beers in her hand.

At that moment I knew it was going to be a good night. Katie told jokes as usual and made us laugh so hard we forgot why we were laughing in the first place. Cassie and Cristina felt the urge to go topless, much to the delight of us male rec. leaders. I can still hear James's ear piercing yells of "Boobies!" years later. Jen, Becky, and BOK spent the night conversing amongst themselves, despite the fact that they were always talking shit about one another at camp. At one point they brought the party down into the basement, where rumor has it, Jen almost made a man out of Joe Voigt. Mike had been given a new name, Big White, because we thought Bud Light Mike would be too much. Cassie and Veronica, overly hyper and intoxicated, jumped in my aunt's pool. Five minutes later everyone else jumped in too.

After his adventure in the basement, and then the pool, I sat at the kitchen table with Joe Voigt and played some card games. He was wrapped in a towel, dripping pool water on the floor. I eavesdropped as Derek, James, and Cesar discussed their usual topic, baseball. The conversation was always a back and forth battle. White Sox fans James and Cesar would team up on Cubs fan Derek regarding some off the wall stat.

"Be honest, you know the Cubs have been terrible for years," Cesar started. "At least the Sox make a run at the playoffs most years."

"Hey be nice. The Cubs went to the playoffs in '98," Derek defended. "And if I remember correctly, the Sox got swept the only time they went recently." He had a strong point but wasn't done, "And the Sox have the most disloyal fans. People only show up when they are winning."

James would never let Derek win an argument, "Do you think the Sox would draw as many fans as the Cubs if they played in Wrigley?"

"No, because Sox fans only come if they win. If they were winning, then yes."

Cesar jumped at the chance to say something. "So it's bad to want your team to win? At least Sox fans want a winner, Cubs fans only care about getting drunk at the games. Wrigley is the biggest bar in the world, end of story."

"Whatever, I hope you guys get shot the next time you go to your shitty ass stadium," Derek said walking away. I could tell he wasn't really mad, but more frustrated that it was hard for him to win a two on one argument. He eventually would set aside his anger, as he and Katie were later found fooling around in the downstairs bathroom.

People began leaving around midnight, knowing that we had work early in the morning. Big White, Katie, and Cesar continued to drink long after I passed out in my cousin's bed. When I woke up to my alarm at seven A.M., I was glad to see the house in one piece.

I stumbled around, looking for sleeping bodies to wake for work. I found Joe Voigt, BOK, Becky, and Jen sprawled out across the basement. I didn't even want to think about what might have happened between a fifteen year old and three older drunk girls. We had about an hour to walk the two blocks to work from my aunt's house. After rounding up the troops, eating some breakfast, and brushing our teeth, we headed off to work just like any other day.

"So I guess you must have had a good party last night?" Julie knew everything before the day even began.

"You should have been there Julie," I told her.

"I would have if I got an invite."

"Really? Next time I will let you know."

"Okay, let me know and I'll be there," she said.

"You better."

When the morning meeting began, I could tell everything was different. The people in the room were coming off as friends instead of coworkers. People I had usually said 'Hi' or 'Bye' to in passing were now people I could hold long conversations with. James, who usually hates everyone and everything, was talking with someone besides the guys. Even though it was just Cassie, and he was still probably thinking about her topless, it was a big step for him. Never before did we all have something to say to each other, something in common to debate, or collective memories. On the other hand, some rec. leaders became part of the group out of default. BOK was all of a sudden talking to Derek, James, and me like we were best friends. We barely even talked to her at the party and apparently she still didn't understand that we referred to her as BOK. I know I didn't have the heart to break the news.

Camp was back to the way I remembered it my first year, just plain fun. I no longer worried about my situation with Leslie. My campers were my top priority again and I insured that by teaching my group as many life lessons, and fun games, as I could think of. I still struggled with behavior management, which left my voice raspy about half of the camp days, but Cesar and I were learning to become coaches for the kids. Our "big brother" approach was only moderately successful, but coaching commands a different type of authority. Unfortunately, the big brother side of me showed up one day during a typical game of pinball.

While Cesar setup the cones and searched for bags for the garbage cans, I arranged the campers into equal teams by the knowledge I always relied on, their ability to play sports and follow directions. Some campers were good athletes, some were good listeners, but very few were both. James's group joined us in the gym and the game began as six rock hard vol-

leyballs soared into the air. Cesar was the equalizer, flip-flop-
ping to the losing team if one side grew a large lead. Balls
were flying like bullets in a Revolutionary War epic, but I was
only concerned with Joe Voigt.

After mocking me for ten minutes plus, I wanted to hit my
counselor with the dodgeball so bad that I was allowing
James's team to build a huge lead. I wasn't going for the win;
I was going for the kill. After a few misfired throws at Joe, I
picked up a ball that just bounced off the rim. I took a few
steps forward to the half court line, causing John Paul to duck
and scream with a pitch I didn't know possible for a boy his
size, and threw a bullet right for Voigt's chest. The throw felt
good, online, straight, and with enough speed the entire gym
filled with the sound of the ball cutting through the air, but he
was quick enough to maneuver out of the way. One camper
wasn't as quick.

(Gene and Julie said time and time again to use soft
dodgeballs when we played. James and I rationalized that
because those balls wouldn't travel as far, hard volleyballs
were needed for pinball's shots across the gym. Besides, the
only people that could cause harm would be the rec. leaders,
and we were never going to be throwing at campers so it was
okay).

The ball hit my camper square in the face and sent him
flying against the wall. The sound of the impact itself was
enough to scare me. When he fell to the ground and laid
motionless, I could barely think straight.

James commanded everyone to stop playing as I ran over
to the dead boy. *This is not good*, is all I could think as I saw
him on the gym floor. I leaned over him and asked, "Are you
okay?"

He was barely moving and was not answering. James
came over and looked down on him. "Did you hear the sound
the ball made?" he said. "I really think he has a concussion."

Concust, as he would forever be known, opened his eyes
slowly but he did not seem to know where he was. He had a

hard time getting the words out of his mouth. "I'm okay," he finally said.

Joe Voigt and I moved him off the floor and into a chair. "Get him an ice pack," I directed. "I don't want his eyes to swell up."

The ice pack was only on for two minutes when Cesar and James began lining up the groups to get their bags for sign out. "His dad will be here soon," James reminded me with an uneasy look on his face. I knew he was worried for me. I also knew he was happy he didn't throw the ball.

Concust and I walked out of the gym and into the hall. He held the ice pack firmly against his head, a common site during camp. What was not common was his inability to walk down the back steps to our sign out spot. He told me he was dizzy so I sent Joe Voigt to get him some water. Before he returned, Concust's dad arrived to sign him out.

He saw his son with an ice pack on his face and shook his head. He was going to ask what happened and I had to be honest. There were too many witnesses around to lie. He took the pen from James and searched for his son's name on the sheet. He signed, put the pen back on the clipboard, and looked at me. I was getting the nervous feeling I hadn't felt since I was caught stealing Magic cards at a Meijer in Michigan. "What happened to him?" he asked me as he tilted his head towards his son. *Game Over.*

"Dodgeball accident. I hit him in the face on accident and he went down hard," I admitted cautiously. "He was pretty shaken up so you might want to keep an eye on him."

Concust's dad looked at his battered son. "It's called dodgeball son. You are supposed to *dodge* the ball, not run into it." He put his arm around him affectionately. "Come on, I'll take you for some ice cream at McDonalds."

"I'm sorry," I said to them as they walked away.

"His dad could have killed you," Cesar reminded me when they were almost out of view.

"You're a good friend," I shot back at him.

In our meeting after work I told the story of how I battered Concust with a volleyball to my coworkers and Julie. She took the incident as a chance to explain how parents can be the difference between a lawsuit and a laugh. Some understood, or remembered, what it was like growing up, and that gave the rec. leaders an edge. She also explained how parents who invest the time into their kids' lives usually raise the ones that are a joy to be around.

I thought about the friends I had and how they interacted with their parents. I knew that Megan's dad would understand if he were in the situation I put Concust's dad in. On the other hand, Derek's dad, who we constantly referred to as "The Emperor," ala Star Wars, would have blasted me with his electricity powers. Either way, Julie was right about parents and I was lucky enough to damage the brain of a "well-raised" child.

That night a group of rec. leaders went out to the Cascade drive-in theater in West Chicago. There was always a double feature playing and by the time the second movie rolled around most people were usually ready for something else. It took me only thirty minutes to want to be anywhere but the drive-in, when Veronica, Cassie, and James abandoned me so that BOK and I were left alone in my car. *This is all just a bad joke.* In a summer when all I had wanted was Leslie, I was now stuck in my car with BOK, who was sitting next to me and all of a sudden silent. I knew something was up, because if there was one thing BOK wasn't, it was quiet.

She moved closer to me and leaned against my arm. *A really, really bad joke.* I was screaming inside but did not know what to do. I went over options in my head. *I could leave, tell everyone what happened, and have her never talk to me again, or wait it out and hope she falls asleep or someone comes back into my car.* I could hear James and Veronica talking outside of the car. Were they laughing at me? Just five minutes before, Cassie and Veronica were in my car. Two fun, cute friends, were my protection. *They left on purpose,* I thought. I needed a plan. Think. BOK grabbed my arm and scooted her entire body towards me so that she was almost on the center console that separated her passenger seat and my driver's seat. Now I understood how Derek felt when we ridiculed him over the belt incident with Jen on Becky's roof. That wasn't real though. Jen wasn't really getting on him, she was probably trying to make James jealous. I was about to be assaulted. Think. *Just scream like someone being kidnapped.* Really I was. *Wait, I got it.* "I have to go to the bathroom." *Genius.*

BOK looked up at me and let go of my arm. She didn't say a word. Maybe she was on to my escape plan. I didn't care. I opened my door and exited nonchalantly before heading to the bathroom. I was so scared she would follow me that I even went in, pretended to use it, and washed my hands. I peaked out the bathroom door before exiting. All clear. As I slithered back to my car, I saw that BOK was still inside. I went over to Cassie who was sitting alone.

"Hey," I said as I sat in the lawn chair next to her. "I'm never going back in my car again."

She looked at me, processing my words. "Why, what happened?"

I glanced at my car, making sure BOK wasn't eavesdropping. "BOK tried to cuddle with me."

Cassie started laughing hysterically. She laughed like Julia Roberts, wide mouth, big teeth, movie starish. "What did you do?"

"I told her I had to use the bathroom." Cassie was laughing louder than before. "It's not funny," I told her. This only turned her laugh into a near screaming noise. "She was holding onto my arm and laying against me. She wouldn't let go. I was so scared."

"Veronica, come ha, ha, here," she said. "You got to hear this." I looked back at my car, no movement. I was sure BOK could hear everything, but Cassie was making the situation feel even more bizarre than I originally thought. Veronica came over, but there were no seats left, so she squatted down between me and Cassie. "BOK just tried to get on Vince." Veronica looked at me with an "oh no" face. "He told her he had to go to the bathroom and left her ass in the car." The laughing began again. "She's still in there!"

"I just wanted to come, watch a couple movies, and hang out." I said to them. "Now I will have nightmares for months."

"I'm sorry Vince," Veronica said consolingly, "you can hang out with us the rest of the night."

"Thanks, but she's in my car. How will I get home?"

"Eventually she has to get out," Cassie said unsure of her words. "Doesn't she?"

"God, I hope so."

Then I thought, *is this how Leslie feels about me?*

I survived the drive-in incident physically unscathed, and transferred the experience into a positive. My patience and strategic thinking were heightened and I used these new skills to maintain order in my group. During football games I passed the ball to every camper. When the group begged to get out of art time I didn't yell and force my hand, instead I made deals with them, exchanges like one hour in the art room for one hour of capture the flag against the girls. I recalled senior year psychology class and reinforcement techniques with surprising clarity. *Where was this info during the A.P. test?*

As the year went by, the kids became more competitive. In particular, Butthole's athletic skills seemed to have grown two fold since last year. He was often matched up against Joe Voigt, and even then he would sometimes prove to be the better player. A big reason I took a liking to Butthole was because I saw a part of myself in him. When I was a camper I played hard in the games and sports each day and believed that maintaining a close group of friends was important. I could see the way in which Butthole talked with his peers, mostly Concust. They became a team, cut from the same mold as James and I were years before. Best friends for six weeks a year, Butthole and Concust were constantly splitting time between being eleven year olds with their friends, and acting as adults around me and James. Never for a second did we think that their attempts to befriend us were outrageous. I remember considering my rec. leaders as more than just guys I saw a few weeks a year. They were part of my life and we shared times that would forever link us.

At first it was bizarre to spend time with Butthole outside of camp, but it was so hard not to want to hang out with him. There were times when he acted like an eleven year old and I wanted to send him to his room or call up his mom and send him home, but most of the time he was just a friend. Plus, it was nice being able to talk to him before and after camp, when the rest of the kids were not around. This allowed me to become acquainted with the person behind the camper, and this was not limited to Butthole. For the greater part of two years I had the same group, and was now starting to build real friendships with a significant number of my campers. I just hoped I would be able to let go when the end of camp came around.

August '02

The last week of camp always fell during the beginning of August, a few weeks before school. Julie agreed to celebrate the end of camp with us, but I wasn't about to let talk of an upcoming party distract me from my job. Still, the last five days went by so fast, it felt as if I was turning pages in a scrap-book of my life. A camp wide game of capture the flag capped what ended up being a hectic final week: one of James's campers got stuck in between two poles on the playground, Butthole inadvertently broke another camper's arm after kicking a soccer ball, and Cassie and Veronica participated in a rainy, midday, mud wrestling match.

When capture the flag ended, a controversial victory for the boys, and the minutes left on Friday afternoon were almost spent, I remained unsure about the party later that evening, one that I was talked into hosting. I discussed it with some of the guys during sign out.

"Do you think we should have liquor if Julie will be there?" James asked Derek when no parents were around.

"I'm drinking," Big White Mike interrupted.

"Okay, but what is everyone going to want to do?" I asked the group.

"Let's not put pressure on the situation. Have cards and some music just in case, and I say we can make a liquor run if we need to," Derek responded.

"Sounds like a plan," James said. "What time?"

"I can pick you up at seven," Derek said, looking at James.

"I guess I'll go there by myself then," Nick whimpered.

"You live three blocks away," James said.

"So do you!" Nick retaliated

"I'll pick you up," Big White said.

"Are you going to be drinking before you leave?" Nick asked.

"Do you think I would do that?" Big White asked.

"Yes," said Nick.

"Fine then, walk you asshole." Big White never understood that some people would rather not risk being in the car with someone who was not only drinking, but under twenty-one at the time. "Vinny, call me and let me know what time."

"Will do," I said as Big White began to walk away.

The rest of my group finished signing out and I could not believe I wouldn't see Concust, J. P., Carlos, and Butthole for another year. Camp was over, and for a second straight year I sat at my sign out spot, dazed. The last sign out of the year. With the evening's party on my mind I didn't really even remember saying goodbye to some of my campers. I looked around at the remaining kids and those walking across the fields to their homes. I didn't even have any stragglers to hang out with. My boys, gone for another year. No more football games in the pouring rain, no more laughing at Julie's morning meeting jokes, no more shouting obnoxious chants with my campers on field trip bus rides. *I wish this job was year round.*

Julie called the rec. leaders in for a quick goodbye meeting but spent most of the time talking about the party that night. "I expect to have some fun tonight," she said. "But, I will not buy you any liquor."

Big White shot a concerned glance at me.

Julie continued, "Vince is hosting so I will pay for some pizzas or something that we want to order." *Too nice.* She looked around the room, possibly checking for questions. "Now, I want to thank you for another great year, but we can talk about all this tonight. Go home and I'll see you tonight."

The goodbyes were brief because most of us knew we would be in touch even after my party. James, Derek, and I walked over to the water fountain by the playground.

"The best water in the world," James would always say. He was right about that.

We talked about baseball, about the end of camp, and about going away to college later that month. James wiped off some leaves from a nearby bench and sat down. Derek and I sat on each side of him.

"When is the last day you can hang out with us before you go?" James was asking Derek the same question for the tenth time.

"My plane leaves that Saturday morning, the seventeenth I think, so I can probably hang out Friday but I don't want to be out that late," Derek answered.

He was going to the University of Arizona for school. Across the country, because he just felt that he needed to. It was hard for me to understand, so I forced myself to believe it was just destiny calling him. He did have some family there but it really seemed like he was going away to prove to himself that he could be on his own. None of us understood why he couldn't "be on his own" at U of I with all of us. James was already settled in there and could ease our freshman transition. Derek was set on leaving, and in a few weeks, our attempts at persuasion would be irrelevant anyway. "How long is the flight?" I asked him.

"Three hours I think," Derek answered. "It's not too bad." James and I nodded our heads in agreement. "See, I will only be three hours away, just as far as you are from Champaign." Champaign, population 60,000, was located in central Illinois, or in other words, in the middle of nowhere. For some people the population wouldn't be an issue, but coming from the greater Chicagoland area with 9 million people, it would feel miniscule.

"It's not the time that will be the problem, it's the money to fly to there," James said.

"Well if I'm not worth the two hundred bucks than that's fine," Derek said.

"Sir? I'll probably be out there every semester," James said. Derek would call this part of the phenomenon known as "James time." According to James, he was always on time, even if he was hours late. He would tell you he would be over in ten and stroll in forty-five minutes later. The best part was when we would ask him where he was all the time, he would get mad at us for asking, never taking the blame himself for being late.

"I'll be waiting," Derek said. "I'm gonna go home and start getting ready for tonight." We stood up and started to walk back to their cars waiting in the parking lot.

Then we heard a voice calling out to us. "Hey!"

"What's up?" James said. He saw Butthole approaching before we did. "Did you go home and come back already?"

"Yeah, home is boring," he said. "What are you guys up to?" It was hard last year to say goodbye, and this year it seemed even harder, for everyone.

"We were just talking about college and stuff like that," Derek said.

"College man, college," Butthole daydreamed. "Are you guys going to be bangin some hot girls man?"

"Derek won't be," James joked.

"What about that Katie chick man?" Butthole questioned Derek.

"Sir, she lives in Chicago."

"Sorry *sir*. When do you leave for Arizona?" Butthole changed the subject.

"In two weeks," Derek told him as we hopped onto the cement sidewalk in front of the field house.

"Yeah, I have school in like a month too. This is my last year until middle school." I was unsure if Butthole was excited or cautious about junior high.

"Who is your teacher?" I asked.

"Mr. Clark man, he makes you say "sir" to him all the time, just like you guys."

"Don't worry, he's cool, I had him back in the day." I hoped my words would relieve some of his angst.

"Okay, good. Hey, am I going to be able to see you guys this school year?"

"We'll come visit you," James said, "at school." We had all stopped by the parking lot and formed a circle.

"Naw…wait for real? You can't come to my school, everyone will make fun of me," Butthole responded.

"Come on, we are the coolest people you know," I said. I wondered if Butthole thought this was true. I cared about his approval more than most people my own age.

"But you guys are so old, they won't let you in!"

"We will tell 'em that we are teachers," I said. *Mr. Tipre has a nice ring to it.*

"I promise we will come visit…and we won't embarrass you," James said in a serious tone.

It seemed like Butthole was unsure of what to say next. "Okay, see you guys later," he decided on. He gave a wave as he turned around to walk away.

"Have fun with the rest of your summer," I said back to him. "That kid definitely makes working at The Park all worth it," I said more to myself than to James and Derek.

"He's a blast," James said.

"Yeah," said Derek, moving towards his car. "I'm going over to Megan's for a few hours. I'll give you guys a call to see what time everything is going on."

"See ya Derek," we said. I said goodbye to James and started walking the one block to my house. Another year of camp over and I really wish it were only just starting. I started to get tears in my eyes halfway home. "Mr. Tipre," I whispered to myself with a smile as I opened my front door. *Why not?*

I was hot and tired from camp and was too lazy to shower when I got home so I jumped in my pool instead. The water was therapeutic. It has a way of making everything serene. I held myself underwater by pushing against the side overhang of the pool; I feel that I do my best thinking there. I was having mixed emotions about the end of camp. It was nice to know that I had the rest of the summer to sit around the pool and eat Taco Bell, but I would miss the kids. I had this *need* to work with them. I swam a couple of laps underwater before I got out. I looked at my reflection in the glass sliding door of my house as I dried off. *Too much Taco Bell.*

I opened the back door and immediately felt the cold of the air conditioner. Half an hour before I would have killed for sixty-eight degrees, but now I was freezing my balls off. I checked the clock, four fifteen. I moved into the living room and sat down on the couch in my towel. My dad would throw a fit if he saw the wet mark I was going to leave. I searched for a daytime baseball game. I am a die-hard Sox fan but I love the game of baseball more than anything. The Sox played at night so the Cubs would have to do. They were surprisingly having a strong year and looked like they could make the playoffs. Big White and Derek reminded me of this fact almost everyday. Lying there in my cool house after a long day, I fell asleep within five minutes.

I had one of those half sleeps where you wake up with a sort of twitch, look around, and fall back asleep in ten seconds. I remember thinking that someone would call me so I didn't need to set my alarm. My body was in that perfect position where sleeping for the rest of my life would be one hundred percent satisfying. The next time I opened my eyes I saw the blurred figure of my dad sorting through the mail. He was just getting home and the front door closing must have woken me. My eyes were too tired to see the time on the DVD player so I hit info on the remote. Five forty-eight appeared on the T.V. I rolled off the couch and saw a big wet mark from my towel. I flipped the cushion before my dad could see and grabbed my cell phone to check for missed calls. "One new message," appeared on the screen. I listened to my voicemail. It was Leslie.

She had not socialized much towards the end of camp, usually leaving right after our meeting and not showing up again until the next morning. I was feeling good about our relationship for the first time in a while. I was not committed to her the way I once was and I think she welcomed this as a chance for us to just be friends.

Her message began, "Hey Vincenzo it's Leslie, I wanted to know what time everyone is coming tonight. So yeah, um, give me a call when you know. Okay, bye."

I dialed her number without the usual nervousness, but she didn't answer. At the sound of the beep I left this message. "Hey it's Vince. James and Derek are coming at around seven, so anytime after that is fine. I will see you tonight. Bye." Simple and friendly. I knew she was going to U of I with me so it was important that we remain friends.

Before I put my phone away I scrolled to "James" and hit send. His cell phone never got reception in his house, but I still refused to call his house phone because his parents hated me. "They hate everyone," he always told me. *Even better.*

When he answered there was static for a few seconds, "Hello Vincent."

"Hey, what time you coming over sir?" I asked to make sure.

"I dunno. I'll walk over at seven?"

"Hawhhwh," I tried to answer but a yawn came out instead. "Sorry about that. Sounds like a plan. Did you already eat?"

"No, I'm waiting for tonight."

"Oh yeah, well I'm going to shower. I'll see you in a bit."

"Okie, see ya."

"Later."

I hung up and spent the next twenty minutes cleaning up my house. Nick showed up first and helped me place some chips, dips, and beverages on my kitchen table. My parents knew I was having people over and they didn't mind. They also didn't know there might be alcohol involved. I felt like such a bad son drinking under their roof, knowing the possible consequences, but I was young and foolish. Everything was up and ready to go at six forty-five, punctuality was one of my best qualities. Derek and James arrived together and I unlocked the door before they could even ring the bell.

"Good evening gentlemen," I said, feeling completely energized for the long night ahead. "How was the walk over?" Derek took off his shoes and sat on the couch, James stood in the entry, not far from Harriet Tubman.

"Hot," Derek complained. "You have any lemonade?"

"I'll get you some, D," Nick said, rising from his seat and lumbering into the kitchen.

"Fuck man!" Derek yelled, responding to the information on Sportscenter. "My team is so bad." Derek had spent the majority of the summer complaining about his fantasy baseball team.

"That's what happens when you pick all Cubs' players," James told him.

"Thank you asshole," Derek shot back.

"James is an ass? I was just saying that," Nick said, reentering the room with two glasses of lemonade.

"One for me?" James asked, reaching for the already perspiring cup.

"I don't think so." Nick handed Derek one of the cups and downed a third of the other. "I love your Dad's lemonade."

"Made with crack," I informed him.

As we sat watching sports highlights and waiting for everyone, Nick, Derek, and I took advice from James about college. We mostly focused on the female aspect of his stories.

"There are so many girls on campus," he explained, "that a good number are bound to be hot." He turned down the T.V., which was interfering with our conversation. He must have been getting to the good part because he moved his body to the edge of his seat. "I would say that seventy percent of the girls are not attractive, so it's not like every girl is hot. But there are fifteen thousand girls at school, and five thousand are still doable."

"I'm down," Derek said.

"All you need is one," Nick clarified. He was king of the long-term relationship.

"Hey, I'll take one," I said. The conversation lasted for about two more outs of the Sox game, or just enough time for my doorbell to ring again. I spotted Cristina and Caitlin on my front porch.

"Be right there," Derek yelled, slowly rising from his spot on the couch. He opened the door, "Come in, come in."

"Hey!" they responded with.

"Hello ladies," I said when the girls made it inside. "Make sure the door is closed because the air conditioner is on."

"Speaking of things that are cold," James said. "Is Leslie coming tonight?"

"No idea," I said. "I hope not," I lied.

My parents were out for the night, so when Katie and Big White showed up with booze, I wasn't too worried. A minute later they began taking shots.

"Guess we are drinking," I said to the group in the living room. "I'm going to join them." I walked into the kitchen and saw Big White with a shot glass in hand.

"That's some good sauce," he commented. He snatched the bottle off the table and read the label. "What is this shit, liquid heaven?"

From the look in Cristina's eyes, she was ready for round two. "It's Bacardi O. I told you it was the shit." Big White lifted the bottle and started drinking out of it. "Hey, don't drink it all."

"I can't stop," he said, slamming down the bottle. "I'm addicted."

The doorbell rang so I went back into the living room to answer it. I could hear Katie and Cristina laughing as the rest of us said our hellos to new arrivals Julie, Cesar, and Becky. By the time I saw Big White again, he was already having his third cocktail.

"What time did everyone else get here?" Becky, who was now sitting down next to me on the couch, asked.

"About an hour ago," Derek answered for me. "James and I wanted to start the party early." He took a sip of his freshly opened beer. "How did you get here?"

"I drove," she said. "My dad was going to drive me but instead I got stuck with the car."

"Just drink, sleep over, and go home in the morning," I suggested.

"Maybe," she replied, then looked up at Big White, who was entering the room wearing his traditional Cubs hat.

"How did you get here?" he asked the room.

"Me?" Nick said, finding Big White's gaze upon him.

"Yeah captain obvious, you." Big White sat on my dad's recliner.

"I walked, it's like four blocks," Nick said.

"You and Joey Voigt man, what the fuck." Big White said disgusted. "He didn't want me to pick him up either."

"Sir, I'm not going to go with someone that is drunk, especially when I can walk. And don't get mad at Joe either," he said.

"I'm Irish, I can't get drunk," Big White defended himself.

"I see you drunk at camp once a week sir," Derek interrupted. Big White gave him a "who asked you anyway look." "How is Voigt getting here then?"

"Fuck if I know," Big White said. "Let me call him."

He stepped into the backyard with his phone to his ear. I asked who paid for the drinks and Cesar told me Katie did. I pulled out a ten and handed it to her. She didn't want accept, but I forced her to take it against her will, and thanked her for picking it all up. We began a conversation about her returning next summer when Julie stepped over and threw her arm around me.

"Are we ordering food or what?" she asked me.

"Sure, La Villa?"

"If you do, make sure you tell them this is an Independence Park party. They will give us our discount," she winked at me and went back to her conversation with Cristina and Caitlin.

"What a boss," I said to Katie. "I don't even have friends that cool."

"I don't even have friends," Katie said to me.

I could not help but laugh. Katie was one of the most personable people I had ever met, and everyone loved her for it.

"I told you to shower more often Katie, once a week is not too much to ask."

"Fine, Vince. Once a week for you," she said. I looked up to see Big White coming back into the house. He was already stumbling over himself. I noticed that it was considerably darker now then when Nick arrived an hour ago. "You look like you need another Bud Light mister." If Katie were saying that to a normal person, I would think Katie was trying to get them to pass out and steal their wallet. Considering Big White's tolerance, he was just getting started.

"Joey Voigt is on his way," Big White said. "I think that dumbass is lost." He continued walking into my bathroom.

I ordered four large pizzas and made an announcement that the party would be moving outside. Everyone shuffled into the yard and found seats on my deck. I took a drink from my beer and sat down in a lawn chair next to Nick and Cesar. We discussed the White Sox for about twenty minutes with James joining half way through. We were hoping this would not be another disappointing year where we are in the playoff race for most of the season but falter in crunch time. Talking with all White Sox fans made me appreciate the love I had for my team even more.

Our baseball discussion turned into talk of starting an intramural softball team at school. James, Cesar, and I all played baseball in high school and felt we knew enough guys to have a strong team. All the talk about playing got me excited for the school year. Nothing takes your mind off of schoolwork and an approaching autumn like fall softball. Well, that and Leslie, who walked into the backyard while Cesar was thinking of some friends he could get to join our team. I tried to concentrate on Cesar's words but was having trouble blocking out Leslie. Her presence was like an itch, distracting and annoying but still somewhat enjoyable. I zoned in and out of the conversation for the next few minutes as Leslie pulled up a seat next to Cristina.

I decided that if we were friends, then I should have no problem saying 'hi' to her like everyone else, so I got up from my seat and walked the ten feet over to where she was sitting. "Hey, how are you?" I started.

"Um, not good actually, but I know you don't want to hear about it," she said.

She was right. The last thing I wanted to hear about was her boyfriend drama. My summer was so much better once I stopped worrying about her relationship.

Cristina said to her, "End it with that asshole and just be with Vince already." As embarrassed as I thought I was going to become, I was now interested in hearing her response.

"It's not that easy," Leslie said back, slightly annoyed. "I have been with him for a long time, and even though we fight a lot I still love him." Her reasoning had not changed for the last six months.

"He doesn't love you Leslie," Cristina responded with attitude, "what don't you get about that? No one that loves you would make you cry everyday, call you names, and threaten you. That's not love."

Leslie got upset at this. I think she felt that everyone was teaming up against her, when everyone thought they were helping. "Can we not talk about this tonight?" she asked, looking at me. She turned to Cristina and said, "I'm going to U of I in less than a month and I will finally be single." Her saying this drew my interest. Cristina tried to respond but Leslie continued. "Besides," she turned back to me with a smiling face, "I'm sure I will sneak into Vince's bed during the year a few times." *Come again?*

I smiled and excused myself to the bathroom to break the seal. I saw Derek hanging out with Becky in the living room and I told him what Leslie said.

"Of course, you're the sexiest man of all time," he said encouragingly. "Just go up to her and kiss her."

"Dear god sir, stop saying that," I told him. I looked at the bathroom door and back at Derek. "Who's in there?"

"James. He just went in."

"So bad," I had to piss like a racehorse. Conversation would pass the time. "So Becky, are you coming back next year?"

She looked up at me from the sofa and gave me an 'I'm not sure' look. "I might work at Oriole Park," she said. "The park that I teach cheerleading at. It's closer."

"Fine, be a hater," I responded. "We will have fun next year without you then."

"Wow, thanks. Hey, your bathroom is open," she said, pointing towards the door. I spun around and saw James headed back outside. Now was my chance at the free bathroom so I hurried in. I heard the doorbell ring and wondered who was here now. When I finished relieving myself I checked the living room but noticed that Derek and Becky were gone. Their voices were coming from outside, so I made a quick u-turn toward the backyard where I saw pizzas being placed on the patio table. I grabbed a few two liters, a stack of plates, and decided to rejoin the party.

Cassie, Veronica, and Ashley were also outside now and were busy playing the card game Shenanigans with Nick. I greeted them, grabbed a few slices, and joined the game. It did not seem possible that six weeks ago Nick had never met these people. He had fit in since day one and also earned Julie's highest approval. Twice he left our game at Julie's request to talk with her privately. I thought of them downing shots together and a hint of jealousy reached the surface. But, I was too relaxed and sedated to think twice about it and continued with the cards.

The few employees who were not yet at my house filed in throughout the next couple of hours. Most parties that I went to were separated by some invisible boundary. At Megan's house it was always divided down the middle, her grade school friends on one side of the room and her high school friends on the other. Tonight, there were no boundaries, as the alcohol acted as a social lubricant to those who never talked at work. I was encouraged that Leslie and I were able to keep having conversations all night without further mention of her boyfriend. I really felt like I had matured so much since the beginning of summer. Having other girls around, like Cassie and Veronica, didn't hurt either. They were good for giving advice about my situation and spending time with them was helping me understand the female brain. I thought I had it all figured out.

As midnight approached and everyone was drunk, Julie proposed a toast. "To the best staff in the world," she said. "Honestly, I love not having to do anything because I have a great staff doing all of my work for me. Cheers!"

"Cheers!" the crowd replied. I chugged my tenth or so beer of the night until it was gone. I spotted Nick surrounding the remaining slices of pizza and snagged a cheese before it was gone.

"You having fun?" I asked him, my mouth half full of food.

"You know," he said, "I'm going to miss all of this. Thanks for helping me get this job. It was everything you made it out to be."

"So that means you're coming back next year?"

"Of course. Every year." I noticed Leslie standing at the bottom of my deck stairs alone, and excused myself from the conversation to join her.

When I hit the ground of my backyard, she told me to "Hold on a second" and she flipped open her cell. Her conversation must have been with whoever was giving her a ride home. I walked around my yard for a minute or two, staring at my old basketball court behind my garage, taking notice of details I never cared about before. Leslie found me back there and gave me a hug goodbye. "You deserve better than me," she said as we stopped hugging. Then she looked me in the eye and said, "I just can't be with you, Vince."

I didn't know what to say. Did she think I still wanted to be with her? Was she telling me she wasn't good enough for me, or was that a copout? I was panicking and said the first thing that came into my mind, "But why?"

She was not happy with my response, or with me. Her ride was waiting and I thought it was probably her boyfriend. "Just drop it, seriously," she said.

"Okay," I mumbled. She turned to walk away. "Have fun with your asshole boyfriend." She didn't even stop.

As I watched her leave, my emotions started to overwhelm me. The empty beer bottle in my hand became my excuse to be alone. I opened the back gate and walked over to the row of large black garbage cans to toss my beer. It was midnight on the last night of camp, I was in my alley, alone, and I just lost it. I was pressured by college, moving away, and now more Leslie bullshit. "This is where I want to be," I whispered to myself. "Fuck school. Fuck Leslie."

Just then Derek came out into the alley.

"You throwing up back here?" he asked.

I wanted to act normal and regroup myself before looking at him. I gave a fake cough and ran my hands over my face. "Naw I'm fine," I said turning towards him. "I had to throw away my bottle and I was just out here thinking."

"Let's just stay and work at The Park this school year," he said.

"Ha," I began. "I was just saying that to myself. Who needs school when you have The Park." I meant it.

"I agree," he said. "But college is going to be so good. The Park wouldn't be the same without camp. No pinball, no Butthole. It would just be you, Gene, and Julie."

"My fantasy," I said.

"Seriously." Derek tried to gather himself in spite of my sarcastic remark. "You would always regret not going to school. No parents. Hot ass girls everywhere. Plus you have James. I have no one. I'm going to Arizona! I should be complaining."

"You want James, you can have him," I joked. "You're right. I just wish U of I was in Chicago."

"And I wish Chicago had Arizona's weather. I'd stay too," he said. "Let's go back in and take a shot."

"Let's do it." I followed Derek into the backyard and saw James jumping up and down like a five year old. He ran over to us and told us his good news.

"Cristina and Joe Voigt just went to Big White's car to have sex," he said. "Apparently she asked Big White for his keys and he said okay."

"What, she's like three years older than him," I said.

"I can't even get with eighteen year olds but he can?" Derek said, which made us laugh.

"Man, what a good way to end the summer," James said. "Little Joey Voigt becoming a man."

James was right. It was the perfect way to end camp. Nick's girlfriend picked him up and James and Derek stayed the night at my place instead of walking home at three in the morning. There were three weeks of summer left until college began. I wanted them to last forever.

Figuring that everyone would be available that first week after camp ended, we planned a trip North Avenue Beach. However, this time around, James didn't have to nearly kill someone for there to be an injury at the beach.

"Holy shit! Are you okay?" Nick may have been laughing but at least he cared unlike my asshole friends. I only remember chasing down the Frisbee and getting tackled.

"What happened?" I was so out of it I thought I might have hit another person. "Why is everyone laughing?"

"You just jumped into that garbage can. It was the funniest thing I've ever seen."

"The garbage can tackled me?" I looked around for the garbage can and could not remember hitting it or how I managed to wind up ten feet from it. "I'm hurting, Nick."

"Where?"

"My hip." I pulled up my shirt and saw bruises, gashes, and blood all down the side of my body. Not bad enough to go to the hospital or leave scars, but definitely bad enough to where my friends should not be laughing.

"Oh man," Nick said.

James ran over, "That was the greatest moment of my life!" He looked at Nick who was not laughing anymore. "Oww, it's really that bad?"

"Worst pain of my life," I said lifting up my shirt again.

"Damn," said James. "Well, as long as you're okay then it's okay to laugh."

Camp had been over for a week, but the beach and White Sox games kept the camp atmosphere alive. Derek, James, Nick, and I spent three nights a week at Comiskey cheering on our mediocre ball club. We went to so many games we knew exactly where to stand for batting practice, how to get Magglio Ordonez to wave to us, and who the best vendors were. We were hanging on to our last days before high school life ended and college began.

Unofficially, the end of summer was Derek's last night in Chicago. It was just James, Nick, Derek, and me, the four best friends. We stayed up all night at my house, talking about high school, camp, and the future. Derek was trying to convince us that he was going to see us all the time, so we had no reason to be upset. I hoped I would be fine without him. He was a brother to me, just like Nick and James were, and it is hard seeing one of your family members move two thousand miles away.

James fell victim to sleep earlier than I expected, so only Nick and I made the trip to Derek's in the morning. The sun was rising over a nearby apartment as we walked down Byron. Derek's dad and step mom were loading the last of his stuff into the car for him as we said our goodbyes.

"Call me when you land later today," I said. "Or at least when you settle in there."

"Sir? You're going to be passed out sleeping until eight tonight," Derek said. We hugged and I began to get tears in my eyes. "I'll call you from my aunt's house."

"Okay," I said wiping my face.

Nick gave Derek a handshake and then hugged him next. "Don't forget about us," he said. "We're all gonna come visit you soon."

"Yeah you bastards are going to come right when it starts to get cold here," Derek said. "Once you feel the Arizona weather you'll never want to come back."

"Well *you* better come back," I said.

"I'll see you before you know it," he said. "My dad's waiting."

We walked out the door with him and he locked it behind us. Nick and I wished him a good flight, saw him toss his last piece of luggage into the back seat, and watched him drive off. His life was now piled into the back seat, blocking the entire back window. "That's safe," I said to Nick pointing at the car.

"They'll be okay," Nick said. We walked down the street to Nick's house, not saying a word.

"Things will be strange now, that's for sure," he said.

"Hey, it will be like the old days, just me and you," I said.

He smiled and began walking up to his front porch. "I'm going to bed. I'll call you when I get up."

"Don't call before two," I said. It was seven thirty-three in the morning when I stepped back into my house. My life felt like a dream. I couldn't believe Derek was already gone and that I would be leaving soon. I said 'hi' to my parents, who were up and making breakfast, and made my way up to my room. I slept the rest of the day.

By the end of that second summer, I understood that The Park was not just there so I could change kids, but so they could change me. My kids taught me patience. Camp showed me how to adapt to situations better and think through my decisions more thoroughly. Plus now, I wouldn't have to worry about Leslie anymore. The University of Illinois was waiting and I only hoped my experiences over the summer had better prepared me.

Year Three

September '02

During my first semester away at school I was happy one moment and sad the next. Jerilyn and I attempted our relationship again but were back and forth most of the time. The tension between us was making life at school over-whelmingly frustrating, so after a few weeks we decided to split for good. I was enjoying my roommate situation with Sean and Edgar, but I still missed Chicago and the city atmos-phere. Wild parties and Jimmy John's at two A.M. were not enough to fill the void.

The first time I came home for a weekend I expected to feel the same way I did during summer. To my dismay, Chicago was no longer the same place without my friends. Derek was across the country in Arizona, James was back down in Champaign, and Megan was at Illinois State. I was without all the friends I had made in high school, but I still had Nick. He was my rock. Best friends since fifth grade.

I found myself at The Park after dark on that first week-end home, a Friday night in September, sitting alone on the same bench Derek, James, and I sat on just a month ago. My thoughts were on Nick and the friends I had known all my life. I met James when I was seven but he was my summer friend. I had very few memories of life without Nick. Family parties, football games, all-night video game fests. Nick, Nick, Nick.

I sat on the bench feeling like I should move back to Chicago. Transfer to a local college and get back to the life I was used to. I pulled out my phone and called Nick.

"What's up Vince?"

"Not much man, what are you doing?" I asked, looking behind me at a group of people walking across our soccer field.

"Sitting at Dale's house. You're in town right?"

"Yeah, you guys wanna get some ice cream?"

Nick must have been asking Dale if he wanted to go with because the line went silent. Muffled noises made their way through the phone for the next two minutes and I wondered if Nick got lost looking for Dale. I made my way over to the water fountain when Nick finally responded, "Yeah we'll go. Do you want to come pick us up or should we meet you there?"

"I'll come get you," I said. "I'm over by The Park and I will leave here in about two minutes."

"Sounds good."

"I'll call you when I'm there. Be ready."

"Settle down sir."

"Bye."

Like the rest of us, Dale lives a couple of blocks from The Park, so after drinking some water and walking back to my house to pick up my car, I was there in no time. I called Nick's cell and he and Dale were in my car in less than a minute, a personal record for both of them.

"Hey there big man," Dale said. He was wearing a new hairstyle I had not seen yet, almost spiked up instead of parted down the middle. He also seemed to have grown three inches since I saw him over the summer.

"Nice hair," I complimented him honestly.

"You haven't seen it?" he said. "People say I look like John Elway now."

"Haha, I can see it. How's school?" Even though we had known each other for years, it was not until last year that we became close.

"It's alright I guess. All these girls are lovin the new hair."

"Dreamboat!" Nick yelled out. "It's impossible not to love you, Dale."

Dale had been given the Dreamboat nickname last school year because of the constant group of girls surrounding him. "How are you getting to school now?" I asked. *Life without a ride everyday must suck*, I thought.

"My mom's been driving me," he told me.

"I love it when your mom gives me rides," Nick said. Joking about having sex with your friend's mom was the kind of humor we were into then.

"She is a cheap, cheap whore," Dale said. Making fun of your own mom having sex with your friends was even better. "And she told me you left your watch in her bedroom again."

"That's where it is. Good, I thought I lost it," said Nick.

We laughed, and I could not help forgetting about the personal crisis I was going through less than twenty minutes ago. I was ready to pack up my bags and come home, but now all I cared about was getting some ice cream with my friends. I turned into the Baskin Robbins parking lot and pulled into a parking spot nearest to the door.

"What were you doing at The Park?" Nick asked as he closed the passenger door.

"Contemplating coming back home," I said. Dale opened the door of Baskin Robins for me and Nick, "Thanks Dreamboat." We stood in line behind an elderly couple that seemed to be debating over what to order. "I like U of I so far, but I just feel like I'm missing out not being here."

Dale was looking at the ice cream flavors through the glass display case. I think he felt that he was not supposed to be part of this conversation. "What are you guys getting?" he asked.

"A shake I think," Nick said. "Probably mint chocolate chip." We moved up in line as the elderly couple received their single scoop ice cream cones. Then Nick said to me, "Well you have to do whatever makes you happy."

"I know. I really just want it to be summer again," I said.

"Oh yeah, I'm working at The Park next year," Dale informed me as Nick ordered his shake. "Nick and I are going to go talk to Julie this week so she can meet me or whatever. I think that -"

"Your turn to order," I interrupted with my finger pointing towards the counter, signaling Dale to turn around.

"Oh, sorry," Dale said to the employee.

"I would say make it through this semester at least and see how you feel then," Nick said to me.

"Yeah, that's what my mom said too," I told him. I knew that they were right, but I just felt so comfortable at home. Regardless, hanging out with Nick and Dale was just the remedy I needed. Ice cream wouldn't hurt either.

December '02

I finished up my first semester at U of I and decided that I wanted to stay. Once the year got going, Edgar and Sean helped fill the emptiness. The three of us were more than just roommates, companions I would call it. We ate, slept, cooked, partied, fought, and watched porn together. *Good times.* When I came home for winter break, I was unsure of what to expect. I had visited Derek in Arizona during October, stayed in contact with the rec. leaders from The Park, and spent time with my other friends on weekends home or when they visited me, but I still knew that things would be different.

A collective 'Hey!' rang out from the group as Derek walked in the front door of Nick's house. Most people had not seen him since he left for school four months ago. He made his rounds, greeting and chatting, and finished by sitting down on the couch next to me.

"How was the flight in?" I asked.

"I slept the whole time, so it was good," he said. "So what's the plan for tonight?"

"Once everyone else gets here, we're going to pick up some beer." Derek gave me a confused look. "Oh yeah, Megan and Keith are both on their way," I answered it.

"Where are Nick's parents?" he asked.

"Out of town somewhere." Nick's parents randomly decided to go out of town a couple times a year, usually taking Stephen with them. That left the house all to ourselves, and Nick was usually willing to have people over.

"Did someone call Keith?" Nick came down from upstairs looking around. "I don't want to wait all night for his dumb ass," he said.

"Make up a list and I'll pick up the cocktails," Big White said.

I walked into the kitchen and found some paper and a pen. "I need money and your order," I requested from Katie, Cassie, Veronica, and James. "So ladies, are you coming back next year?"

Cassie fished into her wallet to find a ten, "I don't think so," she said. "I need to get a full time job."

"I'm definitely not coming back," Veronica pledged with attitude. "I am so sick of that job."

"You just sit around all day. You don't even play with your kids," said James. He seemed to be offended by her comments on not wanting to return. I agreed with him.

"What's wrong with The Park?" I asked Veronica.

"I hate kids," she said.

"That will do it," Katie said. "I want to work there forever but I should probably get a grown up job now that I will be graduating from college."

"All of you will be back next year," I stated confidently. Every year the same people claimed they were done with The Park, and every year we were all stuck in the same hot gym together during training. "The Park is just too good."

"I'm literally never leaving," James said seriously. "There is no reason to ever want to leave that job."

"I always liked you James," I said. "No matter what Derek and Nick say about you when you're not around." He smiled and I picked up the finished drink list and money and brought it into the living room. Megan showed up in the meantime. She was talking with Nick and Big White when I greeted her with a hug.

"What's up Megan?" I asked.

"Not much, did you guys get beer already?"

"Cocktails," Big White intervened, wanting to give Bud Light more credit than it deserved.

"There's a list being passed around right now," I informed her. "What do you want?"

"I'll also take some Bud Light, I mean cocktails." Megan knew the drill by now.

"That will work," I told her. "Cassie and Veronica are getting some hard stuff if you want."

"Naw, beer's fine with me. Hey, Keith is here," she said, looking past me and over at the door.

Unlike Megan, this was only the second time in two years that Keith hung out with my friends from work. Keith was known to make an ass of himself at get-togethers because he had no fear of embarrassment. The previous summer he had stripped off his clothes in front of large groups of people at least three times. For each occurrence he had no regrets the next day.

I handed the list to Keith. His order of 'more beer' completed the list. Big White took the money and left with Katie. Even though Big White had a fake I.D. and had been using it probably since he was fourteen, Katie was actually twenty-one, and always willing to buy us our cocktails.

Megan and I talked about her semester at school and my situation with Jerilyn. I told her we no longer talked, and even though her and Jerilyn were still friends, this came as a surprise. "Well, I guess you can finally be single and not have to worry about Leslie, Jerilyn, Cassie, or anyone else," she said, attempting to show me the bright side of the situation. "Or is there someone else?"

"No, no one else," I told her. "And it feels good. I always put so much pressure on having a girlfriend that my relationships felt forced."

"Well good," she said. "I hope you find someone that is good for you."

"Yeah, thanks. Me too."

Derek was busy talking to Veronica so I felt the need to keep Keith company. He was always good for a laugh throughout the night, either by telling a good joke or being the punch line of one. I watched him as he observed the twenty or so people in the house, then he asked, "Where is the Dreamboat?"

"I didn't invite him," Nick said. "He's only fifteen."

"Yeah, but he's the biggest pimp in the world. Sir, he gets with girls that only laugh at me," Keith said. Even more than making fun of your friend's mom, poking fun at yourself was on the rise.

"That's because they see your small penis," Megan said to great laughter.

"Yeah Keith, are you going to strip for us tonight?" Veronica inquired as she joined the conversation. Veronica was not in our high school circle of friends but even she knew the legend. Her making a comment like this probably made him nervous. Nervous Keith says stupid shit. "If *you* want to see the Donkey tonight, then maybe you will."

Veronica liked messing with him and was not going to back down from the comment. "Oh yeah, 'The Donkey?' That's what you call it? I heard it's really big."

"Nothing can contain it," Keith claimed.

"Nice try Veronica, we have all seen his penis, even small would be a compliment," Nick said.

"So you guys just bust on Keith because you probably have small dicks yourselves," Megan said. "At least he is brave enough to bare it all."

Derek responded in a typical fashion, "Megan, do you want me to whip out the Donkey and destroy this house right now? If you want proof I will do it."

"Okay, do it," Megan and Veronica both said.

"I don't want to murder any of you," was his only rebuttal.

Big White and Katie returned with drinks ten minutes later. We took shots of Vodka, drank cocktails, and made fun of each other all night. Keith managed to keep his clothes on, much to the dismay of us all. Seeing a naked white man's ass in the air always made for a good time. He told me there were too many people he did not know. Stage fright I guess. The night was still a blast. Park employees, high school friends, and new college ones all mingling together.

Keith and I walked the four blocks to my house after the party. We were both trying our bests not to stumble as we passed Frodo's house. His front porch motion sensor lights turned on and the entire block lit up, causing Keith to sprint wildly to the end of the block. Luckily for him the air was surprisingly warm for a mid December evening in Chicago.

"Was that crazy Frodo's house?" Keith asked me, almost completely winded.

"Yeah man, settle down. No need to run."

"I thought it was the cops or something."

"So what if it was?" I questioned.

Still catching his breath, Keith said, "I can't afford to get in trouble with the law. Vince don't be mad, but I just rejoined the military." That killed the mood.

"Sir? The Marines again?" I asked, trying to sober up. I started walking more upright and did one of those head shakes trying to gain some focus.

"Air Force this time. I have boot camp in June." The words were difficult for him to get out. Just six months ago

Keith was supposed to be leaving for the Marine Corp but got sidetracked with girl problems. I never thought he was going to reenlist.

"June? I guess that's not bad. Where are you going to be stationed?"

"I won't know any of that for a while," he explained. "Boot camp is in Texas though."

"It's going to be as hot as balls down there in June."

"You're telling me!" He kicked some melted snow that was left over from the storm we had a week ago. I could hear cars pass on the Kennedy as we approached my block. I wondered how many drunken people were on the highway right now that chose to drive home instead of walking like us.

I fumbled in my pocket for my keys and said, "Well, at least we have six months to live it up before you go."

"Yeah," he said as we walked up my stairs and through my front door.

June '03

I had seen Leslie on occasion that spring semester at school, usually on accident. Camp was right around the corner and I was relieved to hear she would not be coming back. The thought of being with her vanished from my mind. College had taught me that I just needed to enjoy the ride. Cassie, Jen and a few other rec. leaders decided it was also time to 'mail in their retirement papers,' as Big White called it, when they found full time jobs.

With about six new spots open, the entire feel of The Park was in jeopardy of changing. Even more than I could imagine. Before camp started, Julie handed out two park shirts to each rec. leader. I was looking forward to finally having over a week's worth of teal shirts in my closet. When the big brown box, filled with our wardrobe for the next six weeks, was opened at the end of training, I was shocked at the dark green contents inside. Camp was about three things: summer, kids, and teal shirts. Since Derek walked to Nick's house everyday three summers ago, I wanted to wear the teal shirt for every summer until I died. I would bleed teal blood if I could. But if dark green meant a job at The Park, I would have to make it work.

Dale was not going to be working camp either. He was too lazy to fill out the camp paperwork, so he missed registration. That meant that I was not going to have any new friends working this year, which after getting Derek, Nick, and Leslie the job in recent years, was a relief. Camp was already perfect and I did not need to mess things up again.

With one weekend left before camp started, we celebrated Keith's big send off to the Air Force. Big White hosted the event and he simply requested that Keith keep his clothes on. If anyone was unnerved by Keith's nudity obsession, it was Big White.

Keith, Sean, Edgar, and I held four shot glasses in the air. "This is to you Keith," Sean said. Keith, Sean, and I put back our vodka and Edgar downed his shot of water. Besides being a light drinker, Edgar was the designated driver for the evening.

With a few more shots in our stomachs, Keith called over Derek and Megan. He wanted all the Lane graduates together one last time before he left. "Can we do a shot for high school?" he asked us. I eyed Sean because I felt another shot would do me in. He grabbed his shot glass without a second thought.

"Hell yeah Keith," Derek said. "Anything for you."

"Forget Keith, this shot is for *Lane*," Megan said. One hour and one too many drinks later, Keith was sitting on Big White's sofa buck-naked.

"Keith you are an asshole, you know that right?" Big White complained. He was talking not only for himself but also for the thirty or so friends that had gathered to say good-bye to him.

Keith replied, "Everyone loves seeing me naked. *You* love seeing me naked."

"Inappropriate. No one here wants to see you naked."

"I do," James replied. Big White gave him a disapproving look. James ignored him and looked back at naked Keith. "You are the sexiest man alive."

"Thanks James," Keith said. Then he bent over so his head was almost touching his knees. Interestingly enough, people were still sitting next to him. Conversations were not put on hold when his clothes came off. "I'm going to throw up."

Big White was nice enough to let people stay even though the guest of honor was puking all night. We convinced Keith to put his clothes back on before Edgar, Sean, and I threw him in the back of my car and drove him to my house.

In the morning we ate some cereal and I had to retell him the story of how he took off his clothes in front of thirty of his closest friends, many of whom were unaware of his naked affliction.

"At least I'm going away tomorrow," he said optimistically. We were sitting on my couch trying to relieve our hangovers from the night before.

"You have a point there," I said, changing the channel on the T.V. "Come on, I'll drive you home." Neither of us had any intention on ever leaving my couch, but nevertheless there were errands he had to run before he left. We slowly ascended from the couch and put on our shoes. I made a quick run to the bathroom and met Keith out by the car. We both got in and rode off discussing his future in the Air Force. He convinced me that the next four years would fly by fast, and no matter where he ended up being deployed, we would remain close.

Keith was my best friend that did not work at The Park, and a good counter balance to my camp friends. He left for boot camp in Texas the next day. I would see him only a few times for the next four years.

The next week camp began and Joe Voigt and Caitlin, both of whom were counselors in the past, were now old enough to be rec. leaders. Caitlin split a boys group with Derek, but Joe Voigt was left in charge of a group on his own. Not surprisingly, he did not take his job seriously. On the other hand, new rec. leader Grace, my camper Gabe's sister, was a hard worker. Knowing the pain the ass her brother was, I felt sympathy for her from the get go.

Then there was Dale, and even though he wasn't a rec. leader, I was able to talk Julie into letting him volunteer at camp. He needed community service hours for school and this gave him the best opportunity to get a feel for camp without having the real responsibilities of the rest of us.

"So I'm good to go? Still, I won't get paid," Dale brought up to Nick.

"Settle down. It's better than sitting on your ass all summer," Nick said.

"Fine, I'll do it," he said. "What time do we start?"

"Well it used to be ten, but now kids get there at nine. Employees at eight thirty," I told him.

"I already hate this job," Dale said.

Nearly all of the twenty something year olds retired and were replaced by sixteen year olds. I became a seasoned veteran overnight. On the first day of camp another sixteen year old new employee, Jaimie, made an impression.

"What are you reading?" Big White asked her. She was sitting outside with her group as they ate lunch.

"Get the hell out of here," she said back to him, focusing her eyes back on *Harry Potter*.

"Don't kill me," Big White said as he walked over to the hot dog stand.

Lunchtime at camp meant eating outdoors, brown-boxed lunches, trips to the hot dog stand, and one big mess afterwards. I have not been to the hot dog stand since I was in camp, but from what I hear, I am not missing out.

The hot dog stand was stationed just a few feet off of Irving Park Road. Teddy, the man who has run the half car half restaurant for over a decade, can be seen taking regular trips to the bathroom before serving his customers. That wouldn't be so bad if the bathroom at least had soap in it. You would think that he would at least put on latex gloves, but he didn't.

Sweaty Teddy, as he became known over the years, was a smelly, disgusting, foul man, who would rather swear at kids than serve them. I could not imagine day camp without him.

"The new girl just told me to 'get the hell outta here,'" Big White said as he shoved down half of a hotdog.

"Who, Jaimie?" I asked. Big White nodded his head as he took another bite. "What did you say to her?"

Big White chewed for a couple more seconds before swallowing. "I just asked her what she was reading and she told me to go fuck myself."

"Haha, she really said that?"

"No, but she did hurt my feelings."

"Yeah, I don't think she likes any of us, or this job at all."

"I think she is on the rag," Big White said, looking in Jaimie's direction. "She is reading *Harry Potter* too. What is she ten?"

"No joke," I said. "Do you think she will go to the drive-in on Friday?"

"Only if she gets to bring her book with I bet."

"She probably would," I assured him. I walked over to the dumpster and threw away the lunch that my mom had made me. Left over pizza, Doritos, and a cold Pepsi - my favorite. I spotted Nick leading his group out of the park house. The boys were in two perfectly straight lines as if Nick was a drill instructor, but there was not one face without a smile on it. James and Derek had joked that Nick was the perfect rec. leader, and times like this were proof. As he led his group onto the field he asked them questions, "Who wants to play dodgeball?" and "Should we race to the tennis courts?" to thunderous replies of "ME!" and "YES!" I joked to Big White that the kids were so perfect for Nick because they were terrified of him.

Big White tossed his hot dog wrapper into the dumpster. "I can't even make one kid listen to me," he said. "I think it's because of his dirty beard. All of you White Sox fans and your dirty facial hair."

"Whatever man. But seriously, I swear you can hear them chanting 'Nick, Nick, we love Nick!' as they walk past."

Big White pretended to listen for the words as I checked my phone. It was time to bring the group to the gym. "Let's go eleven and twelve year old boys, it's time for gym!" I hollered so no one could use the excuse that they didn't hear me.

"See you later Vinny," Big White said.

"Yeah," I said back. I turned towards my group and saw the mess they had made. I noticed Cesar with some of our boys at the water fountain so I had to take charge. "We are not going anywhere until all of this garbage is picked up!" my now booming voice echoed off the field house. A handful of campers began looking around and grabbing pieces of garbage, the rest just ignored me.

When the garbage was all picked up we went into the gym and started a basketball tournament. Four captains picked their own teams and Cesar and I decided that they were even. But, as the week went on, I was impressed with how well Butthole's team played together. He was acting as the captain and coach at the same time.

John Paul, who was by far the biggest boy in the group at age eleven, was the only competition for Butthole. The championship game was Thursday, and their two teams were in the finals. While John Paul was able to grab most of the rebounds, he could not get his teammates involved enough to have a real chance against Butthole's team. I crowned the champions at the end of gym time and we made our way to the

pool for our last event of the day. This time when I saw Becky
in the hallway with a sinister look on her face, I already knew
what she was going to say. "Pool's closed, there has been a,
well, you know."

"Really?" Joking or not, I was tired of our pool.

"Afraid so."

"Okay, thanks Becky." She smiled and went back into the
locker room where her girls must have been changing. I followed a few stragglers into the boys' locker room and broke
the news to my group. With the tournament just ending, it
could not have come at a worse time. "But you know what,"
I did some quick thinking, "you can still change into your
trunks if you want and we can go to the sprinklers." The boys
normally acted too cool or old for the sprinklers, but they
were not passing up the opportunity to cool down. Five minutes later my campers and I were drenched from head to toe,
my khaki shorts and dark green camp shirt included.

July '03

The basketball tournament ended just in time, because the
next day was the only rainy day of the summer. Whenever the
sky opened up to fulfill the thirst of the land, our field got the
worst of it. The two main softball diamonds became mini
lakes and the playground transformed into a water park.
Chicago Park District policy forced us to stay inside, but our
park house was too small and ill equipped for two hundred
campers. That day we were spared the tight squeeze because
the rains came in the morning. A large percentage of campers
opted to stay home, leaving just six kids in mine and Cesar's
group.

A recent argument in schools is that small classrooms can
improve the quality of education immensely. Rain day proved
to me how true that argument is. Cesar and I took our group
to the auditorium for most of the day, where the eight of us

shared stories and laughs. Neither Butthole nor Concust were there that day, but I think that helped me learn so much. I was always picking favorites with my campers, seeking out the best athletes and funniest kids because that's what I thought camp was about. After spending the 2003 rain day with an oddball group of campers, I knew that every single kid had something to offer and I would never have favorites again. Besides Butthole.

Rain day also brought about a revelation in our fight to even the score against the lifeguards. For three years the life-guards mocked us with their unhygienic pool. Knowing that Gene and Julie forced the rec. leaders to go in the water, the lifeguards relished the times when feces were expelled into the pool. BOK's interest in one of the lifeguards, known to us only as 'Hates Life,' became perfect fodder. Everyday he would contemplate killing himself by jumping head first into the pool with no intention of surviving. At least James and Derek decided that's what he was doing as he sat on the side of the pool deck everyday, staring blankly into the water for hours upon hours.

"Is he studying the cracks at the bottom of the pool?" James joked.

"Whatever it is, it must make him so sad," Derek added. "I hope he doesn't go through with it. Suicide is not the answer, not even to get away from BOK."

"Oh man I hope he does!" James exclaimed.

I tended to label James and Derek's antics as immature, but it really did seem like he was contemplating some serious issues on that pool deck.

My parents broke some bad news to me over that week-end. They decided to put our house on the market and move into one of their real estate project houses. The news came, but my sister Mercedes and I were not going to leave without a fight. My brothers had moved onto to their own places, so for years the house was just me, Mercedes, and my parents. We were mad at them for wanting to move away from the only home either of us had ever known. My life was in that house: our pool in the backyard, the smell of chocolate chip pancakes in the morning, memories of waking up Christmas mornings and seeing the tree surrounded by presents. And The Park. Very few days of my life went by without me walking through its grass or sitting on its benches, drinking from the water fountains or throwing around a baseball. A part of me. I began to have my doubts about the move. Would The Park still be as important to me if I no longer lived a hundred feet away?

I decided I needed to have a sendoff party, so when my parents went up to our house in Michigan for a week, I invited everyone over for one last summer get-together at my old place.

I talked about the party during that next week, inviting people, getting drink orders, and fine-tuning any other details. Because I was careless, and overall didn't really mind, Butthole found out about my party.

"Can I come?" he asked during lunch on Wednesday.

"No way Butthole."

"Why not, I'm old enough to party."

"I don't think it would be appropriate."

"Just ask James. If he thinks it's a bad idea, then I won't ask again."

James thought it would be a fantastic idea, and I am weak willed, so Butthole got invited.

"You cannot invite a twelve year old to your house," Cesar said. "You're gonna end up in jail."

I had a new policy that included not playing favorites with my campers, so if Butthole *was* coming to my house, he was *certainly* not allowed access to the beer. "I'm not going to let him drink. If -"

"You're not?" James cut in. "I wanna see that kid drunk!"

"Sir?" There was too much at risk. If Butthole was going to be around then I had to keep an eye on him.

"Look, Butthole's tapping the keg!" Sean yelled. It was five hours later and I had thought, *Hey, I can't get this thing to work, maybe a twelve year old can.* Big White and James cheered us on, and sure enough beer was flowing a few seconds later.

"The day is mine!" Derek hollered from the table in a Scottish accent. He was obsessed with Sean Connery's latest movie and was stuck on reciting the two quotes he heard in the trailer incessantly. "That was naughty!" I wasn't sure if he was complimenting us or not.

"That was cool man," Butthole said. "I'm going to tell my mom how much fun that was."

"Sir, you can't."

"Aw Vince man, I was just kiddin'," he laughed. "Beer tastes nasty anyway." His comment did not surprise me. I grabbed some red cups and started to fill and pass out beer with the help of Sean pumping. James called Butthole over to him. He said something in his ear and then I heard Big White say to James, "Dude, you're going to end up in the big house." *This can't be good,* I thought.

"What? It's nothing," James said.

"Fine, just bring more attention to the twelve year old at the party," Big White said.

Over the next ten minutes Butthole walked around my house asking for donations. Before he left for home, he was going to jump in my pool with all of his clothes on as his finale. Not surprisingly, my friends donated over fifteen dollars to the cause. A group gathered round my pool and Butthole prepared for the jump. He ran towards the edge but stopped a foot away. He turned to me, "You got a towel for me?"

"Yeah, right over there," I said pointing to a stack of towels sitting on a bench.

"Okay, good, good." He walked back to his starting point. "Okay, I'm going this time." And off he went. The crowd cheered for his flawless cannonball. He emerged from the water shivering, "Shit Vince! It's cold." He waded over to the ladder and climbed out. His clothes looked ten pounds heavier. "Man, this was a stupid idea. James man, I want a refund."

"Okay, I'll give everyone back their money," James said.

"Naw man," Butthole's face was half anger half confusion, "that's not funny, I was joking."

"I know, I know. Relax," James told him. I brought Butthole a towel and he started to dry off. "Here's your money."

"Thanks everyone, I hope you enjoyed the show." Butthole waved to the smiling crowd. Half the people had no idea who this kid was but that made it even better. Butthole asked for the time and I told him eight forty-five. "Oh shit, I'm going to be late. My mom's gonna kill me." He put the towel down and put the money in his pocket. "Okay Vince, good party. I'm going to go home and see if I can skateboard by Murphy."

"Alright Butthole, thanks for coming. Put your clothes in the dryer right away or they will start to smell." And he was gone.

BOK and Hates Life appeared at my house just after ten o'clock. I walked them into the kitchen to show them where the Bud Light filled keg was. Most people saw the two of them walk in together and we wondered: who would crack first, him or her?

"Imagine them having sex," James whispered to Derek.

"I don't want to," Derek said.

"Picture it!" James started making moaning noises, "After they do it he would kill himself because he Hates Life so much."

"That was naughty," Derek said.

"Okay Sean Connery, we get it, you are only famous for one liners," James replied.

"Come on James you don't know. Maybe they will be happy together," Cesar said. He was still on a high from his new romance with Grace.

"Are you picturing it, Cesar?" James screamed. Now even BOK and Hates Life were looking over.

"Why do you call her BOK?" Grace asked us.

"BOK BOK BOK BOK!" I shouted as I jumped up and down, alternating feet, my arms flailing between my legs. The BOK dance, as it was known, was always funnier when intoxicated.

"Not that dance again," Cesar said. He acted embarrassed by us, but we knew he was just too uptight to show his true feelings, that he loved how stupid we were.

"BOK BOK BOK BOK!" Big Obnoxious Kristin yelled. "Why are you guys always saying that?"

"Because Vince and James are stupid," Cesar answered her. I wondered if he would have the same opinion if Grace weren't around.

"You love it Cesar, you know you do," said James.

"Yeah, yeah," Cesar said lifting his red plastic cup up towards James. "Fill this up for me yeah?" James took the cup and placed it under the tap.

The moving out process had already begun. I looked around at the bare walls of my house. "Doesn't it look weird in here?" I asked Derek.

"You can't move man, this is like my second home," he said. James walked over to give Cesar his beer before joining us. "James and I were just talking about what we are going to do now everyday after camp."

"And what about when you have to take a shit and you usually run home?" James asked.

"No joke," I admitted. "I'll just have to teach myself to

shit in the public toilet."

"What about me?" James said. "Where will I shit when I have diarrhea?"

"We can use it together in the basement bathroom," I said. "Hold hands underneath the stalls."

"Promise?"

"Promise," I said. "But seriously, the new house is not far away. Let's go check it out tomorrow." I could tell by their faces that I was much more excited to see the house than they were. "Or not."

"We'll see," Derek said. "Still, I am going to miss this place. Remember when Keith mooned your brother on the back porch?"

"Haha yea, good times. I miss that guy," I said. "Fuck it, let's do a shot right now for Keith." I walked over to the freezer to find some hard liquor. I reached in and pulled out a bottle of Jagermeister. "Who wants a shot?"

"Pour that shit Vinny," Big White said as he walked into the room. I swear he can hear the sound of liquor being poured from a block away.

I laid out glasses and red cups in front of me and must have poured at least ten shots. "For Keith," I said raising my cup.

"Keith!" James yelled.

"My little naked boy!" Derek said.

We downed our Jager and I washed out the cups. I spotted Caitlin and Cesar talking. Something she said made him get up and walk into the living room with her. The buzz was starting to pick up and it was only ten thirty. Ashley and Veronica walked into the room with cups in their hands. I never even saw them come into the house.

"I think Caitlin is leaving," Ashley informed the crowd.

"Really?" I hurried towards the front door and saw her walking down my front steps through the screen. "Why are you leaving already?" I asked her.

"I have to be home at eleven," she said. I barely talked to her all night and felt like she was leaving because she was bored.

"Oh," I did not know what else to say, but I felt bad. "I'm sorry you didn't have more fun."

"I had fun Vince. I actually had a good talk with Jaimie all night. I just have to go."

"Someone can walk you home," I told her.

"Jaimie's mom is driving me," Caitlin said. I noticed a dark figure standing outside by a waiting car. "See you Monday."

"Yeah. Goodnight." I watched as Caitlin stepped out onto my front porch and joined Jaimie in her mom's car. I didn't know how they could be leaving my party while Ashley and Veronica were just arriving. I guess that was the difference between high school and college girls.

I reentered the kitchen and took a seat next to Ashley. I grabbed my beer and joined in on the card game already in progress. "So you're moving?" Ashley asked me.

"Yeah, my parents have made up their minds and I'm tired of fighting them on it."

"Isn't that going to be weird?" she asked. "You won't be able to run home during lunch and pick up food anymore."

"I know! That's the biggest reason why I'm mad. But I guess it's for the best. I'm gone away at school most of the year anyway, so it's not a big deal."

"Don't let him tell you it's not a big deal," Veronica said. "The new house will never live up to the expectations of this place."

"Yeah, yeah," I mumbled.

"Seriously Vince, we have all had so many good times in this house," she said, as if I needed some kind of reminder. "Like that one time we were all drinking in your basement and Keith took the full beer can and smashed it on his head."

"Is that your friend that is always getting naked?" Ashley asked me.

"Yeah that's him. He had blood dripping down his face. He was never the sharpest tool in the shed."

"Why isn't he here tonight?" she inquired.

I gave her a look of confusion, then figured there was no real reason she would know. "He left a few weeks ago to the Air Force. He's in Texas right now."

"Oh. Well that must suck," she said with empathy. "Do you miss him?"

"Everyday."

James had started dating a girl from school over the winter named Joanne. His relationships were always a mess so I was unsure how this one would work out. But, as James told me, "For the first time ever, I actually like the girl I'm dating."

"It's about time," I told him. If anyone could understand what he meant, it was me.

"I really do feel like I have found a girl I deserve," he said.

"Sir? You are the sexiest man in the world, no girl deserves you."

His facial expression told me I was an idiot. "Have you seen me? I am an ugly, ugly man."

"You're delusional. You are a good looking man." He was. "Besides, Joanne is cool, I mean she plays *Smash Brothers* with us, you know you have a keeper."

"Yeah, you're right. Thanks."

"Anytime."

Joanne had become a friend of mine during the school year, so when she would come by The Park a few times a week to pick up James after work and not say "hi" to me, I was offended. I didn't need her to strike up a conversation with me, but a simple wave would have been nice. Our friendship seemed to disappear as quickly as it had formed.

During a week four sign out I was talking with Caitlin and Cesar when I spotted Joanne parking her car by my house and walking towards us. "I bet you James just leaves with her without saying bye to any of us," I said, watching him closely as she reached his group.

"Let the guy be happy," Cesar said to me as if I was hoping for James to fail. "So what if he goes with his girl."

"It's just that he never answers our calls anymore," I elaborated on my first comment. "You know, we used to all hang out everyday and now we see him maybe once a week. And it's not that we hate Joanne, because we don't."

"Who is 'we'?" Caitlin asked.

"Me, Nick, and Derek I guess. They always have to be alone and that's fine, but James always hated his previous girlfriends so it's hard to see him spending all of his time alone with her," I said.

"Sounds like you guys should all sit down and talk," Cesar spoke as a voice of reason.

"I'm sure he would not be acting the same way if he knew how you guys felt," Caitlin added.

Our conversation was put on hold when a parent approached to sign out one of my remaining two campers. "Hey there," I said. "We have a field trip tomorrow to the zoo, so make sure he wears his camp shirt and that he brings a lunch."

"Okay, what about money for the gift shops?" the mother asked me.

"We should have time to stop there, so that's up to you," I said as she signed him out on my clipboard, which had overtaken the binder as the most important tool in the rec. leader's arsenal. Everything became simplified the more comfortable I felt running my group. It was a wonder how fast the binder became just another lost accessory down in the meeting room. The mother motioned her son over to her. "Thanks Vince, see you tomorrow," she said as they walked away.

"What were you saying Caitlin?" I asked apologetically.

"Tell James how you feel," she said.

"I know, I will…soon."

My last camper signed out and I made my way down to the meeting room for our after camp talk with Julie. The meetings usually ran about ten minutes and then we were all free to go. I used to hate sticking around just to hear the recap of the day's events or to go over tomorrow's activities, but now I enjoyed the comfort and familiarity of it all.

"Where's James?" Julie asked looking around.

"He has one kid left," Cesar said.

"Okay, we will wait for him," she said. I looked at Cesar and shook my head in disapproval of James's actions. Even if he did have one kid left I knew he was going to blow off the meeting and leave with Joanne. Cesar shrugged his shoulders back at me and went back to his conversation with Grace. He told me their relationship was going really well, but because he was a few years older, he didn't know what would happen when he left for school. I was thinking, *I could never do a long distance relationship,* when James entered the room. "Nice to see you join us," Julie said to him.

"What do you want me to do? I had one kid left," he said defensively.

Julie gave him a forgiving look. "Lincoln Park Zoo tomorrow everyone!" Why did she have to remind us? "I know we all love the zoo."

"I quit!" Grace yelled out.

"What would you know? This is your first year," Julie said.

"Well from what my brother Gabe tells me, I quit."

"The zoo is the best," Big White said. "It's hot and smells like the men's locker room."

"That was naughty," Derek added in his best Sean Connery.

"Oh yeah, so good. There aren't even any animals there," Katie added. "Half of the cages are empty."

"Yeah Julie, when is Gene ever going to spend the extra money and get us some good trips?" BOK asked. For the first time she and I were on the same page.

"Hey, hey, hey. We have a small budget and the money we get is spent on radios, balls, and other new equipment," Julie enlightened us. "The field trips we find are just as fun as other ones, *and* they are free."

"Some of them, yeah," BOK replied. "But the zoo Julie, can't you just get rid of the zoo trip?"

As much of a goofball as Julie was, she was not as amused as the rest of us. "Come on, the zoo isn't that bad. So tomorrow, make sure you bring water bottles, sun block, and a marker to number your campers. And I think that is it." She checked her clipboard for any more notes she may have made. Most of us stood up and began folding up our chairs. "Oh, one last thing before you go. You have less than two weeks before the talent show, so you better be practicing." I surveyed the room for worried faces. Somehow the talent show snuck up on half of the rec. leaders every year. Not me.

The zoo trip began with a bang. Veronica was absent during the morning meeting and Julie asked me to call her to see where she was. "Hello," she answered her phone, "did you guys leave for the trip yet?"

"Not yet," I responded, "but the buses will be here soon. Where are you?"

"Well, I actually am on my way. You will never guess where I slept at last night."

"Apparently not at home. A homeless shelter?" For Veronica, I could see it happening. "I dunno, where?"

"At the apartment of a certain Chicago Cubs' second baseman and catcher."

I ran their roster through my mind. "Are you serious?"

"Haha, yeah!" She was so proud of herself. "I met them at a bar and they invited me and my friends to hang out with them."

"Wow, that's amazing, and really not that surprising. But really, the buses will be here soon, so hurry up. You can tell me the rest of the story when you get here."

"Okay, see you soon."

Veronica showed up to camp as the buses were pulling away. For her, being late wasn't uncommon. Showing up drunk was. We arrived at the zoo, and shortly after eating, we split up to begin our tour. I took a group of six kids while Cesar and our two counselors divided up the rest. We walked along the outside pens of elephants, camels, and buffalo, stopping for a few minutes at each to examine the size of the crap piles each could make.

"One time, after I ate some Chinese food, my crap was as big as that," Concust said pointing to a very large camel turd.

Soon after comparing shit sizes and colors we stopped in the primate and small animal houses. A few campers went downstairs to use the bathroom and I used this opportunity to talk to Nick who was walking by with a group of his boys. We discussed our plans for the White Sox game James, Derek, Big White, and the two of us were going to after camp. Even though everything with James had changed that summer, it was nice to be able to mention his name without some criticism or doubt following.

My campers finished in the bathroom, and when we were ready, we left the small animal house and made our way over to the polar bears. The size and strength of bears fascinated me, so this was always one of my favorite parts. I was disappointed when the lone bear's only action was repetitiously moving his head in a circle, as if trying to bite his own ear. After five minutes of hoping he would entertain us with something more, we sped off in search of a place to rest with some shade. I spotted Veronica walking without her group. "Where you coming from?" I asked. My small group of campers found a spot to rest on a nearby bench.

She appeared to be looking around, for who I did not know, then she sat on a bench across the main pathway from my campers and glanced at me. "I'm so drunk. Not even hung over yet, still drunk." I eyed my campers to make sure they did not hear her. "I just want to go home and go to bed."

"Where's your group?" I asked her. Now I was looking around, for her group and for Julie.

"I don't know." Her face told me that she was too sick to really even care. "I left them with my counselors. I think the sun is making me feel ten times worse."

I looked over at my group to see if they were getting antsy waiting around, but they seemed to be enjoying the rest. It was extremely hot, probably high nineties with almost no cloud cover. "Do you want me to get you some water or ice or something?" I asked, eyeing the nearest beverage stand.

"No, I'll get it," she said, slowly rising from the bench. She walked over to the stand and I cut across the crowd to my group.

I noticed that some of my campers were missing. "Hey, where are Gabe and Concust?" I asked the rest of the group.

"In line for pop," someone answered. I sat down on the bench with my group and was glad they had chosen a spot with some shade. I turned my head to locate my campers when I noticed Veronica, around the back of the stand, leaning over into a garbage can. I was very grateful at that moment that I was not in her position.

Gabe and Concust were coming back over with large drinks in their hands. "What's wrong with Veronica?" Gabe asked. "Is she hung over?" Clearly he knew a little too much for an eleven year old.

"She's sick," I said with some finality, not wanting the group to discuss her drunken state.

"She's hung over," Concust said, agreeing with Gabe. The two of them took their seats on the now crowded bench.

I turned to the group, who were all looking at my sick friend. "Listen guys, Veronica is not hung over," technically the truth, "and you can't just say that because not only is it not true, but if it was, she could get fired."

"Why would she get fired?" Gabe asked. "People always go to work hung over, don't they?"

"I'm sure people do, but not if you work with kids for a living." I saw Veronica back in line for water so I figured it was time to finish up our zoo tour. "Let's go over to the Cat House." The group replied with a disgruntled moan but stood up nevertheless.

Our entire camp always met by the sea lions before we left. We followed Julie's lead and walked back through the zoo, revisiting each exhibit in glances like flipping through a school yearbook. We found our buses right where we left them and boarded in the same manner we had exited. Derek, Caitlin, Cesar, and I double-checked our numbers and we okayed the driver to take off. Two minutes later Gabe had stripped off his clothes and was prancing up and down the aisles, swinging his shirt in the air as we made our way down Lake Shore Drive. Even the bus driver was amused, turning up the music at one point when Gabe requested it. Carlos, Concust, John Paul, and Butthole all cheered on his rendition of Madonna's *Like a Virgin*. Throughout the ride all I could hear over the music was Derek's constant montage to Sean Connery. By the end of the trip I think he said 'the day is mine' twelve thousand times.

The zoo trip is infamous at camp because of the repetitive, boring, and free-for-all nature it encompasses. Every few years one of our campers will get lost in the mass of people, cry because of the heat, or almost fall into the seal tank. As my group exited the bus and sat down for sign out, I was thankful for another zoo trip to be over with, and all I could think about was Gabe's dancing and Derek's Sean Connery voice. I didn't really care about his new movie, but Derek's damn quotes were stuck in my head worse than an 'NSync song.

Derek came over by Cesar and me to discuss plans for the rest of camp. Scavenger hunt and talent show ideas for the campers, and an end of the year shindig for the employees. I sat down to rest my feet and turned to form a semi-circle with Derek and Cesar when Butthole came over and turned us into a square. "Hey Derek man, can I ask you a question?" he said. We all listened closely because Butthole was not one to ask permission for anything. "Who is 'the Danish Man?'"

"The Danish Man?" Derek asked quizzically. "Umm, I don't think I have any idea what you're talking about."

"Come on man I'm serious. You talk about him all the time."

"Is this a riddle or something?" Cesar asked.

"No guys, I'm serious." Butthole said. "You are always talking about 'The Danish Man,' and I wanted to know who he is. Everyone laughs, but I don't get it."

"When do I ever talk about him?" Derek asked.

"All day today. You kept saying 'The Danish Man' 'The Danish Man.' Like every minute. I don't get it." Derek and Cesar were lost, but just then I finally understood

"Haha sir, it's not 'The Danish Man,' it's 'The day is mine!'" I explained.

Derek and Cesar finally understood the mix up. Derek's face went from confused to excited in a matter of milliseconds. Cesar just looked disappointed that Butthole was asking about something completely arbitrary. "THE DAY IS MINE!" Derek yelled. "It's a Sean Connery line from his new movie."

"Oh man, I always went around saying 'The Danish Man,'" Butthole said. "No one ever corrected me."

"They do sound exactly the same if you say them the right way," I added. "Wow, you have got to tell James that, Butthole."

"Really?"

"Yeah, ask him 'who is the Danish Man?'"

He looked at me, unsure if I really wanted him to go ask, so I encouraged him with a "go" hand gesture. "Alright, I'll be right back," he said, and he walked the fifteen feet over to James's group to ask him the sixty four million dollar question.

August '03

As camp approached its final week, Dale was still volunteering. He had already finished his community service hours, but kept showing up in an effort to form a good rapport with Julie. He wanted to improve any chance he had on getting a paid spot next year. While Frodo and Stephen were spending another summer sleeping in, swimming, and playing basketball, I was proud that Dale was trying to be responsible.

My biggest worry was the dreaded talent show. It was less than a week away, and even though Cesar and I had had our group practicing for most of the summer, I was on edge. I had become obsessed with turning the traditionally worst part about the camp year into the most memorable for the campers and myself.

I couldn't get Butthole to participate because he was one of the few who got stage fright. He said that the song I chose, "Elephant Love Medley" from *Moulin Rouge,* was a little too much for him to work with. J. P. and Gabe had no problems with the song and stepped in as the two lead roles. Skinny Gabe was our Satine, thick J. P. played Christian. I choreographed a routine where the boys danced with each other. Half the group had to be females for the show, so bringing in wigs and dresses was going to be key.

There are only so many times twelve year old boys can hear a sappy love song until they start singing along. It was even better to witness the dance steps and verses being practiced during games of dodgeball.

"We should be lovers!" Gabe would sing.

"We can't do that," Carlos would sing back, narrowly dodging a ball from Butthole.

Gabe hollered back even louder, "We should be lovers! And that's a fact!"

Seeing my boys transform from love hating adolescents into singing and dancing hopeless romantics was unforgettable.

By the time the last day of camp came along my boys had transformed into Broadway stars. We were the last group to perform for the talent show, and we watched a half dozen other acts before us to gain some confidence.

"Everyone is so bad," Concust said to Cesar. "They don't even have costumes."

"That's what me and Vince have been telling you. All that practice is going to pay off."

The music for the oldest girl's group ended and we could hear the applause. "Okay boys, it's your time to shin," I said, trying to calm their nerves. "Just relax, remember what we practiced, and have fun."

I put in the *Moulin Rouge* CD and watched as my boys began their performance. I tried to plan the dance so that the audience would not get bored, an important aspect of the talent show the other groups always overlooked. The crowd laughed and clapped at all the right places, and in the end, not only did my boys execute the routine perfectly, but not one heel was broken.

"That was your best show yet!" Cristina said to me after we walked off stage and down into the art room.

I could hear the applause from the crowd of hundreds of campers, parents, and guests in the audience. "Was it really?" I asked her. I knew that it was good, but I couldn't predict the reaction.

"I laughed my ass off," she said. "Where's my brother?"

"Downstairs changing." I guessed Carlos was where he should be, but with that kid I never really knew.

"Well I'll just talk to him later about it then."

"Okay."

My boys were so relieved to be finally done with the act that they could not help smiling. Most of them were talking about how much everyone was cheering. Grace came into the art room to congratulate her brother.

"Gabe, I never knew," she said. "At least all that singing at home was worth it."

"We got the biggest applause by far!" Gabe said. "They loved looking at me in my sexy dress." He caressed his body like a stripper, all too well for an eleven year old.

"I think you should stay a girl," J. P. told him.

"I think you're right," Gabe said.

Grace looked at her brother one more time in full costume and smiled. "I should get back to my group," she said. "Parents are waiting." She left the room for our last sign out of the year.

"Look at my sexy titties!" Carlos said running into the room with his dress half off. "They're real too." He was right about that.

"Hey, hey, hey listen up!" I was struggling to get everyone's attention. "John Paul, Concust, please."

"Sorry," Concust said, now quiet and attentive.

"I wanted to say that I am proud of you guys. I know it was a lot of practice but I hope you had fun working on the show. I know I will never forget this."

"Where do you want all the costumes?" Cesar asked me, picking up after the boys.

I eyed the lot on the ground, "Boys, make sure you take home any costumes you brought. Your moms and sisters will not be happy if they can't find their pantyhose." The boys started sorting through the mess of clothes that laid on the floor. "When you are done, go with Cesar outside for sign out."

After ten minutes of helping my campers change and find their possessions, I walked outside to join the group. Only a handful of campers remained, namely those who were going to find it hard to leave camp for another summer.

"I'm going to come back as your counselor next year," Butthole informed me. I had already taken stock in the fact that he was one of the few campers I had my first year who was now too old for camp. "Is that okay with you?"

"That's okay with me Butthole." He gave me a quick hug before walking across the field on the way home.

"Camp will be strange without him next year," Cesar said, clipboard in hand.

"Yeah it will," I replied. I changed my position so that I could see the small group of remaining campers. It was J. P., Carlos, and Gabe. "You boys will all be back as campers next year right?"

"Come on Vince, you know this camp can't survive without my sexy body," Carlos said.

"I'm here every year," J. P. said.

"You know it," Gabe added.

"Well, at least there was still some hope for next year," I said to Cesar.

"You call that hope?" he said, eyeing Gabe and Carlos who were now molding their stomachs into various shapes.

"Yeah...that's the best kind of hope I could ask for."

The middle of August always had a strange feel. Camp was over and I would never walk the one block to work again, but summer still had a few surprises left in it. James, Nick, Dale, Derek, and I gathered at The Park on a Saturday to have a homerun derby. We setup in the tennis courts because they were best fit to handle our contest, with a fence to determine homeruns and lights at night to keep the balls visible.

James was the most consistent homerun hitter, even though he was the smallest out of all of us. He knocked ten over the fence in the first round, out slugging almost everyone else put together. I walked to the water fountain before Dale started off the second round. The water was so perfect, cold and plentiful, with just a hint of iron. Indistinguishable. When I opened up the gate to reenter the court, I saw Butthole talking to Derek. He was holding a bat and telling Derek to pitch him the ball. Butthole had promised me on the last day of camp that he would be back next summer as my counselor, and even if he didn't I hoped that we would still keep in touch. I guess he didn't want to wait long to make an appearance. In reality, whenever he showed up it was like a guest appearance of some big name actor on a sitcom. We were all decent characters in the world, but Butthole would steal the show. For those thirty minutes or so he would make life that much better. Then he would be gone, and the audience could only hope his next cameo would be soon.

When I got closer I could hear him begging Derek to let him hit. "Pitch the ball. Come on, just one time Derek, man. I will only take one swing I swear."

"Get out of here," Derek commanded. "You're so bad and you're interrupting our derby."

"I'll leave you alone if you just throw me one. One swing only."

"Fine, one swing." Derek wound up and threw Butthole a pitch at twice the speed he was throwing them to the rest of us. It didn't matter. The ball was sent flying over the fence, continuing above the Women's Building, and landing somewhere near the street for a homerun.

A collective uproar followed with Derek falling to the ground as if he just lost the World Series. Butthole waved his hand in the air with his head looking down. Respecting his fans but staying humble. Butthole, our king.

Another year gone by but this time camp would never be the same. The week after we derbied I cleaned out my old room, packed up my life, and moved into my new house just before I left for my sophomore year at U of I. This year Derek lingered in Chicago just as long as everyone else and we all planned on leaving the same weekend for our schools. Nick,

Derek, and Megan met up with James, Dale, Big White, and I at our favorite restaurant, Lou Malnati's, to say goodbye to another summer. We ordered our food, two large pan pizzas, and joked about another summer that had ended so suddenly.

"Man, I wish I would have worked this whole year," Dale complained. "And gotten paid."

"Next year man," Nick told him. "You better not hate again this time."

"I won't, I'll sign up the first day," he said.

I smiled when I saw the pizza. This day was a sad one but it still was ending the summer on a positive note. I took a bite of the hot cheese pan slice and looked around at my friends. "Next year we will be the old guys. Becky's not coming back, BOK is leaving, thank god. That means we are officially the oldest rec. leaders," I said.

"Besides Katie," Derek reminded me.

"Oh yeah, I forgot about her."

"Maybe Megan will join us," Derek said turning to her. "You know you want to be part of The Park rec. leaders."

"I think hanging with the rec. leaders once a week is enough for me," she said. "But thanks for the offer."

"If only you knew the power of The Park," Nick said as he poured some parmesan cheese on his pizza. "If only you knew."

We split up the price of the food and said our goodbyes to Derek and Megan as they were headed off to school the next day. I would not be leaving for two more days and I planned on seeing the other guys again before I left.

I dropped off James and Dale at home and headed back to my house with Big White riding shotgun. I pulled up in front, turned off the engine, and got out. My new house was big, but I was having a hard time adjusting. Everything felt out of place, including the side of the street my house sat on. I was an east side of the street guy now. My whole world seemed backwards.

Big White closed his door and joined me on the sidewalk. "Next year, Dale can take my place," he said randomly.

"What do you mean?" I asked, hoping my interpretation of what he was saying was wrong. "At The Park?"

"Yeah Vinny, I'm mailing in my retirement papers." Big White walked over to his car and I followed him. He slid his key into the trunk to unlock it.

"You're really not coming back?" I looked back and forth between Big White and his trunk. If anyone loved The Park more than me it was Big White. "Everyone says they are done, but they always sign up for one more year. You know that Mike."

Big White opened his trunk and pulled out some pieces of paper. They were forms of some sort. "I joined the Air Force last week," he said. "I'm going to be leaving this winter for boot camp."

I was completely perplexed. "I didn't even know you wanted to join the military."

"Well I need to do something with my life, Vinny. I fucked up away at school and I don't want to sit around on my ass for the rest of my life."

"What did your parents say about it?"

"You are the first person I told," Big White said. "I'll let everyone else know soon."

"Why are you telling me?"

"You're my guy Vinny, and I know you won't give me shit for doing it."

I felt guilty because I did want to give him shit for it. He was one of my best friends and we only had good times together. A sort of fairy tale friendship. He closed his trunk and started walking towards the driver side door. "It's just weird. I was having this exact conversation with Keith about eight months ago. When do you leave?"

"Beginning of January," he said. "Don't worry, I'll see your ass before I go."

We gave each other one of those half handshakes, half hugs. "I'll call you when I come home for a weekend," I said, releasing my grip.

"We'll have some cocktails," Big White said.

"Anytime Big White, anytime." I started walking up the front steps of my new house. I was still having trouble calling it my home. "Good night."

"Night Vinny," he said as he closed his car door.

I fiddled with the key for a few seconds before I managed to unlock the door. "Damn Mike," I said to myself as I stepped inside. The last thing I needed before I headed off to school for my second year was knowing that I would be missing out on time with another friend.

Year Four

September '03

James and I were now roommates at school with two other friends. Even better was that friends of mine from freshman year, including Sean, lived across the hall. I could have fun with the crazy guys across the hall and still come back to my own clean apartment where my real roommates lived. I felt like I had the best of both worlds. The sinners and the saints.

My camp money was not going to last me through sophomore year. My parents paid for my food and housing year round, but the two thousand I made every summer was not enough to sustain my extra needs anymore. I needed a constant income so I could go out for dinner or buy the latest DVD I wanted. When I nailed down my class schedule, I decided to search for a job that could fit into my free time.

I wanted to get into the education program at school, so a job working with kids was my goal. There were always job ads in the school newspapers and websites to look at, but I never had to bother. A friend of mine worked for the after school programs of Champaign elementary schools. I was timid at first about applying for a job where I now had to work with kids in a school setting.

I applied and was accepted on the spot as an activity leader for an after school program at Garden Hills Elementary. The kids were younger than at camp, from kindergarten to fifth grade, but it was my first chance to work with girls. I knew I needed to expand my work experience if I wanted to be a teacher. Day camp was a good start, but I figured my new job would be even more beneficial.

Over a roommate dinner the first week of class I told James about my new job. He seemed interested enough to ask how he could apply. He was already debating switching his major from pre-med to English. He also wanted to continue to work with kids, and an English degree coupled with a minor in education would qualify him as a high school English teacher. He deliberated with Joanne about this change of majors over the first weekend of the semester. Mostly he was scared of his dad's reaction. Whether it was because he didn't want to be a doctor anymore or that he was probably spending an extra year's worth of tuition on school, his dad would not be happy with him. Regardless, James switched his major the next day.

I was skeptical after the first couple of weeks about my roommate arrangement. I thought I was going to be living with one of my best friends; instead I was living with a guy named James and his girlfriend Joanne. Joanne spent most of her days at our apartment. James spent most of his days locked in his room with Joanne.

When we did talk it was about the after school job. I told him where to go to fill out the applications, and he relayed the information to the also interested Joanne. I had my first day of work but they were still in the hiring process, both wanting to know what kind of questions I was asked during my interview, how much the job paid, and what responsibilities I had. I hoped that James would get hired at my school. We had an open position, but I was too new to recommend anyone for a job.

That semester I started my first classes that would help get me into the College of Education. It was comforting to be on an actual path towards graduation instead of caught in a web of classes. I found that my one class, educational psychology, was far more enjoyable than my general education courses. I loved that my professor would assign writing topics about child development, where I could write about my own experiences growing up or situations I encountered working at camp.

The last Friday of September was the first time Nick came down to visit me and James. James had just been hired to work for the after school program and was ending the first week at his new job. I was off of work, so as soon as James got home, the three of us were ready to go out. We picked up Joanne and went to dinner on Prospect Avenue, where most of the city life in Champaign existed. Nick followed our directions and turned into Cheddar's parking lot. He parked the early nineties, two-door mustang his uncle left to him when he died. I undid my seatbelt, opened my door, and hopped out, pulling my seat forward so James and Joanne could squeeze through the door.

"We should stop at Meijer before we go back to your place," Nick said to me eyeing the bright red sign of the superstore.

"If you want, you're driving," I told him. Nick had visited me regularly at school freshman year, so he was somewhat comfortable with driving around town.

"Yeah, we can pick up some food for the weekend," he said. "I don't want to eat all of your food." It was nice that he was willing to pay for the food that Joanne ate everyday for free. Nick looked back at James and Joanne, "Where do we go in?"

"Keep walking," James answered.

Nick held the door open for the three of us and I approached the hostess to see how long the wait would be.

"How many do you have?" she asked.

"Just four."

"We can take you now, please follow me." We walked to our booth, sat down, and received our menus. I ordered last, my usual, the Chicken Caesar Pasta Salad, and asked for water as my drink. As we waited for our food, Joanne told stories about her first few days at the school she was recently hired at. This was all news to me, considering I didn't even know she followed through with the application. Still, Joanne was never shy about making conversation with us, so waiting for our food was just as fun as if Derek was with us instead.

By the time the food arrived our talk had changed to teaching. James told Nick how pissed his dad was that he changed majors, but how he was finally happy with the direction he was headed.

"The hardest part was telling my dad I didn't want to be a doctor," James said before he took a bite of his burger. He paused to chew, then continued, "He acted like I decided to become a drug dealer or something. Like teaching was such a lackluster profession."

Joanne was eyeing James as she sipped down her water. "That's how a lot of people look at it. You know the line, 'If you can't do, teach.'"

"It's sad that teaching probably used to be like that," I said. "I had many teachers that simply told me what page to look on and what problems to answer. Nick, you remember Mrs. Rowe."

"So good!" he said.

I laughed at his remark and finished my thought, "The material wasn't being facilitated, but like, commanded."

"I know, I just hate when people look at me like that when I tell them I am going to teach," Joanne commented. "Most people think it is an easy profession, but it's definitely not." She tried to snatch a fry from James but it was touching his ketchup. "People can be so ignorant."

"It's not my fault you don't like ketchup," James defended himself.

"Not you," she said, "people who think they understand teaching."

"Oh," James said.

"I couldn't agree more," I responded proudly. Not only was I surprised to find out that Joanne wanted to be a teacher, but I admired how adamantly she believed in the field. I went back to working on my pasta salad as James and Nick discussed the Cubs' chances in the playoffs. They both agreed they would be out in the first round.

When the check came we added up our totals and searched our pockets for a means to pay. Debit and credit cards were not overwhelming popular yet, so a thin stack of cash was left with the bill.

We picked up some snack food at Meijer before we ventured back to our apartment. Joanne went back to her place, which left the three guys to hang out all night. My other roommates were either working or asleep by the time we got back shortly after ten. Before we even took off our shoes, James had turned on *Super Smash Bros Melee*. The game pitted Nintendo characters such as Mario, Yoshi, Link, and Kirby, against each other in a free for all fighting match. The three of us played non stop for the next two hours. Nick and James were left battling it out for second place most games. Because I owned the game, and it was basically the only game I played, I was almost unbeatable.

Nick and James were each down to their last lives when a lucky game glitch in James's favor killed Nick. "That's bullshit," he said angrily. "Next one is my last, I'm sick of this game and I'm about to pass out."

"Okay," James and I said approvingly. It had been a long day and I needed to get some sleep.

We played our last match and it took twice as long as normal matches, as it always did, because no one wanted to lose the finale.   James tended to stay away from the battles between Nick and me while he powered up and tried to sneak in for the kill. Once I finished off Nick, he went straight into my bedroom to get some clothes to sleep in. He came back out of the room ready to sleep, blankets and pillows in hand. James and I were still playing. In the end, his hit and run style prevailed, as I couldn't overcome the number of lives he had.

"Goodnight gentlemen," James said as he walked down our hallway to his room.   "Night." I turned off the game and put the controllers away. I stood up, "Good night, Nick." He was already laying down in the fetal position. I think I heard him mumble good night back to me.

That night I laid awake in bed thinking about school, work, teaching, and just about anything else there was to think about. I wondered if Leslie was back at U of I and if I would see her this year. Or even worse, if I would see Jerilyn. School was big enough so that I could go the next three years without passing by either one. *Time would tell*, I thought, as I dosed off into a set of dreams I couldn't recall in the morning.

On Saturday James went out early to Joanne's.   We wouldn't see him for the rest of the weekend. Instead we spent our time with my 'other roommates' across the hall. Nick was always up for anything, so we went out to the bars with Sean that night. In Champaign you only have to be nineteen to get into the bars but twenty-one to drink. It is true that the bartenders, bouncers, and cops enforce these rules, but there is still not much stopping you from getting drinks from your older friend, or even more likely, one with a fake I.D. For all intents and purposes, the drinking age at U of I is nineteen.

Sean was a barrel of fun all by himself. Nick and I thought of him as a cartoon character. Not only because he sounded like one but because he was without regard for his own safety and others' feelings. There was nothing he would not do, including cheat, steal, and light his own carpet on fire.

The guy even got beaten up freshman year after he started throwing rocks at some upperclassmen that were hanging out on their balcony. He was the human version of the Tasmanian Devil. Even more important than his wild side was his knowledge of the bar scene. He told us what drinks to order, how much to tip, and even what to do if the bar got raided.

The three of us were drunk so early that we left the bar an hour before it closed and picked up a cheese pizza from Pizza Hut. We brought the pizza back to Sean's place. He pulled some Pepsis out of the fridge and we watched *Van Wilder* as we ate. I don't remember the trek back across the hall, but Nick and I made it back to my apartment to sleep. Unlike the night before with my mind racing, I drifted off to bed drunk and carefree.

The morning was a hangover, literally and figuratively. Nick had some homework to finish so he left after the Bears' game. I walked him to his car and we talked about James and how frustrating it was to have him around on Friday and then not show up or return our calls on Saturday. Nick loaded up his trunk and gave me a hug. Not the way you see two guys hug where they pat each other on the backs like it is 'too gay' for men to touch, but the way brothers do. I reminded him how to get home and told him to call if he got lost, but he would be fine. After he left I went back to my empty apartment on the eighth floor. I didn't want to sit around by myself, so I walked across the hall. Sean was watching football and I took a seat next to him on the couch. I was getting that feeling that comes every Sunday: when you have homework still to do and the weekend is ending. Your fun is over and reality begins to settle back in.

I would become frustrated again with James and Joanne without having Nick around for support. I had other friends at school but none like James. I'd known him my whole life and thought nothing could come between us. I just never had a friend who wanted to spend every minute with his girlfriend.

It hurt to know that one girl could change over ten years of friendship.

I avoided the uncomfortable apartment life by spending most of my time after class at Garden Hills. Being an activity leader involved generating a great deal of activities and my camp experience only helped so much. Preparing snacks and organizing games for the kids was familiar to me, tutoring them was not. I went to my coworker Emily for advice, and she gave me some valuable insight.

"You'll realize that most of the time the students will act helpless, when really they are lazy," she said. "Work on a few of the problems together to boost their confidence and then make them do a few on their own."

"Okay, but sometimes they act like they can't do the work at all," I said helplessly.

"They're just so used to their parents doing their homework for them that they just say that." Emily wasn't even an education major but she still had experience I didn't. "Give them some help, then make 'em do it themselves. That's what I do, and it works."

While her input did not always produce the perfect results, I was starting to build a base of teaching knowledge. I learned the specific differences of kids in different grades. How second graders were still dependent on others to tie their shoes and help with homework, but third graders yearned for independence. Or how kindergarteners were mostly at school to become socialized. I could even tell you that cursive writing begins in second grade, and division begins in third. The transformation from a rec. leader into a teacher was underway.

December '03

By the end of the semester James and I had a love-hate relationship. I knew that I needed a change or I was going to lose control, and lose a friend. My last final was over but I still had to stay at school and work. With no real reason to be in my apartment, I spent every waking moment across the hall, where I felt more welcome than my own place. On Wednesday and Thursday night, to kill time in between work, Sean accompanied me to the bars. We hit up the usual, KAM's and CO's, because the cover and specials were both cheap. The liquor shrunk my problems with James each evening, only to resurface with a hangover in the morning. Finally, Friday came, and my final day of work with it.

My last after school session before winter break was a memorable send off. There was snow on the ground, but the weather was warmer than it had been, so my coworkers and I decided to take the kids outside for free time. I tossed the football around with some of the older boys. The fifth graders were only a year younger than my boys at camp, but they were nowhere near as good. Going to camp every summer probably had a much bigger impact on their athletic skills than I thought. I was chasing down the ball after an errant kick from one of the boys when my coworker Emily came over to me.

"Look at Nicholas," she said, pointing over my right shoulder, her mouth half covered so no kids would hear.

I picked up the football and glanced to where she was pointing. I saw six year old Nicholas but couldn't tell what he was doing. He was standing by a group of trees, away from the playground where the rest of the kids were. I threw the ball back to the boys and told them to throw it to each other. Emily tugged on my jacket and started to laugh. I turned back to Nicholas and couldn't believe my eyes. He was squatting over in the 'I'm about to take a crap' position. I squinted to be sure.

"Is he - ?"

"I think so," she answered. "I saw him doing this a minute ago when I came and got you." We both were staring at him and his peculiar position.

He was about a hundred and fifty feet away from us, but right then I saw it happen. "HE JUST SHIT!" I said excitingly. "I saw it! What do we do?"

"I'm not going over there," Emily said pushing me towards him. "You go talk to him."

I looked at her like she was crazy and then focused back on Nicholas. He was picking up a stick. He inched it closer to his butt. "He's going to use it to wipe," I said, hoping I was wrong.

I wasn't.

Emily and I slowly walked over to him, making sure no students were around. "Nicholas, what are you doing?" Emily asked, trying to avoid looking at the pile of brown feces.

"I had to go to the bathroom," he said without hesitance.

"How come you didn't ask us if you could go inside?" I asked him.

"I really had to go and it was just too far," he retorted.

"Nicholas, go inside and wipe yourself off with toilet paper," Emily commanded with a firm tone.

"Okay," he said lackadaisically, still not ashamed of or embarrassed by his actions.

Keeping a straight face was the hardest thing I ever had to do. But I managed, because I knew that laughing in front of him could have been traumatic. Heck, I still remember how embarrassed I was after wetting myself when I was in preschool. I was terrified to tell my teacher, but when I did, she made it seem like it was no big deal. My confidence for the rest of my life could have been greatly altered if things went slightly different that day. Still, I felt that Nicholas wasn't going to develop any sort of complexes over the incident, so I marked it down as a success.

Two hours later I headed home for winter break.

I called up Big White when I got up that next morning to see him before he left for boot camp. We had to postpone our farewell until just after the holidays. We met up, drank a couple cocktails, and talked about his plans for the future. He wanted to be stationed in the U.S., complete his four years of duty, return to Chicago, and maybe even use the degree he got going to technical school. "Fix furnaces or air conditioners," he said.

"I'm gonna miss having you around," I told him.

"Vinny, you turning gay on me?" Big White never wanted to hear that kind of stuff. "Seriously though, don't worry about me. In a couple years you're going to be a teacher. You've got everything planned out...just stay away from that Leslie chick."

"I promise to stay away."

"Good," he said.

It was hard saying goodbye to another friend.

I used to think I was the one who left. The one who had it bad living in the cornfields of Illinois, two hours from home. Now, the drive from Champaign to Chicago wasn't too bad. I had visited people across the country and knew people across the world. Derek, Keith, and now Big White, they were the ones far from home. I could come home on weekends to see my family or Nick could visit me every week if I needed him to.

I lived close.

I was the lucky one.

A week before the spring semester began Sean informed me that one of his roommates was transferring out of school. There was an open room in his apartment, and it was being offered to me. Though it was a hard decision to make, when winter break ended, I moved out of my apartment with James and across the hall. My third move in the last six months. I questioned if my life would ever be stable again.

May '04

The after school program's end of the year roller skating field trip made me look at all the camp field trips from a different point of view. Unlike our summer trips to the beach, zoo, or Field Museum, there was not a disappointed kid in sight. From what I could tell, roller-skating was cheap and simple, both characteristics Gene and Julie considered a priority when they scheduled our park ventures. I debated bringing it up with Julie, but there was something nostalgic about camp field trips that I was scared to change.

It had been years since I skated, but spending one last day with the kids at Garden Hills was enough motivation to try my best.

"Mr. Vince, are you going to come back next year?" a fourth grader named Alexandria asked me as I helped her lace up her skates.

It had taken me a while to get accustomed to the semi-formal name, but now I could not envision how I worked at camp without it. "I hope so Alex, but I won't really know until August."

"Well I hope you come back next year." Her words made me proud of my work throughout the school year. I learned so much, from both class and work, that I felt like I could take on the whole world by myself.

She looked down at her newly tightened skates, "Can I skate now?"

"Yeah, you're good to go."

"Thanks Mr. Vince." I smiled and watched Alex skate off to meet her friends.

"Anytime."

College summers begin in early May, when you pick up your life from the last nine months and move it back home, wherever that may be. For locals, such as Nick, you only have to sell back your books and clean out your car of schoolwork. Those that go far away to school, like Derek, have to store or ship everything that won't fit into a couple of suitcases and carry on luggage. For me, it was just one full carload and a two-hour drive home. Summer had begun.

I was not looking forward to a summer living in a new house and now making a morning drive to work. And even worse, I would no longer be able to walk my neighborhood and wind up at a friend's house. I felt disconnected.

Veronica returned home from school in Iowa and hanging out with her was at the top of my priority list. For some reason I again developed feelings for a girl who could never think of me as more than a friend. I hoped that being in close proximity with her would force the issue, but as the early days of summer went by, I realized how much I had changed since Leslie.

Subsequently, I took some time off from girls to hang with Frodo, who was recently kicked out of St. Ignatius for vandalism, and Stephen, who was just skating by with below average grades at Von Steuben. They were finishing up their school years, Frodo now at St. Pats, with no plans for the upcoming summer. Both had talked all year of working at The Park but neither had the initiative when it came time to sign up. Dale, on the other hand, did apply for camp this time around, and it was great knowing one of the younger guys was following in our footsteps.

It was hard, but I had to accept that Frodo and Stephen had their own hobbies and circles of friends now. They were both independent of me, which hurt at first, but then I came to realize it was a positive. We still spent weekends hanging out, talking about college classes versus high school ones, relationships, Magic, and girls, always girls. I didn't have to mold them into younger versions of myself, but rather help them mold themselves.

June '04

In June, Keith made his first trip home since being stationed in England. He resembled the old Keith I remembered from high school, which was good, because I could only take so much of 'Serious Keith.'

We planned a get-together at my house on his first night home. Keith was already tired because of the jet lag, but promised to make it through most of the night. He only had two weeks in town and wanted to make them last. We chatted about his responsibilities on the base. He asked about Leslie.

"She left school and I have not talked to her," I told him. "What about you? Are you seeing anyone?"

"Naw, well not really," he gathered the words to say. "There is this one girl ...but we're just friends."

"I'm sure it's tough anyway, with people going off to war or changing bases every year or two."

"Hell yeah. It's almost impossible to have a relationship. Plus the military is only like five percent female."

"Well, you only have three more years."

"I know! I can't believe it's been a year already."

"Time flies," I said, going over to my fridge. "You want something to drink?"

"Just some water man." I pulled out two cups and started to fill them with ice.

"I like the new house," he pointed out.

"Yeah, me too. Still getting used to it. Gotta drive to camp now."

"Oh yeah, so bad. So who's coming over? Camp people?"

"No. Why would they come?"

"I thought you always hang out with them."

"Not always, but I'm not inviting people you don't talk to."

"I wouldn't care, invite them if you want."

"Settle down sir." I set down the drinks and flipped on Sportscenter. We began talking about the baseball season that was nearing its halfway point. Derek, James, Edgar, and Megan all came over to greet Keith back to Chicago.

"I have to ask," Megan said the moment she sat down, "how many people have seen your ass in Europe now?"

"Wow, nice to see you too," Keith responded. "But if you must know, no one."

"You are maturing right before my eyes," she said.

"I wouldn't go that far," he said. "I'm just waiting for the right time. They aren't ready for the full moon."

"Be gentle on them," Derek mentioned, "they haven't had time to prepare for your ass."

"It is a grand occasion," James added.

"I'm not sure if I should be flattered or ashamed," Keith said.

"Ashamed," Megan replied.

"Flattered," Edgar corrected.

Throughout the evening we took pictures, ate Wendy's, and played *Super Smash Bros*. Keith talked about his training to become a sniper and the chances he would get deployed to the war in the Middle East. I could never imagine him fighting in war, but not because he wasn't capable. When I looked at Keith I never saw a bloodthirsty killer. He was just too smart…and goofy. Yet, his new duties as a sniper were right up his alley. He was still trained to kill, but it was efficient, professional, and technique driven, not chaotic, rapid-fire mindlessness. Still, as I continued to hear more stories during the night, I remained fascinated by his dedication to his craft.

"For training we had to stay in one position for hours in pouring rain waiting for our shot," he told us.

"How far were the targets?" I asked him.

"Five hundred yards at least. Sometimes a mile or so."

"How accurate were you?" Edgar questioned.

"I didn't miss," he said, "which is great, especially considering the targets might only be a few inches."

"You are my hero," James said. "Remind me to never get you angry."

"Well, at least not if he has a sniper rifle in his hand," Derek added.

We caught up on each other's lives for the next few hours before Keith informed us that it was time for bed. "Alright guys, I would really like to stay all night but I am exhausted," he said sometime around one thirty in the morning.

"Get some sleep and call me tomorrow when you are refreshed," I said to him.

"We should go to Lou Malnati's tomorrow," Derek suggested while everyone found his or her shoes.

"I'm down," Keith said, "just let me know when."

"Good night," I said to the leaving crowd of people. A few scattered 'good nights' were returned to me as I shut the door. I could hear their parting conversations outside as I climbed my stairs for bed.

The next two weeks were a trip down memory lane. I didn't realize how much I missed waking up to Keith's phone calls and always having someone around to waste away my days with. He was usually up for a good time, suggesting bowling or shooting pool instead of just sitting around my house every night.

He left a few days before camp training day, and I couldn't believe it would be another six months or so before I could see him again. Life was just bland without Keith around, like a Captain Nemo's Sandwich without their secret sauce.

By the time training came around, I could tell that Katie had distanced herself from the rest of us. She was a college graduate now and was teaching all throughout the city, hoping to find her own classroom come August. Being that we were the most involved with The Park, James, Nick, Derek, and I were now going to be 'in charge' of camp. Becky, BOK, and Big White Mike were gone, camp felt changed.

Luckily, James was finally starting to come around. I think he missed hanging out with the guys. Training was one of the few times in months we saw James without Joanne being there. Derek was not one to confront James about the situation, so when he told him how he felt as we sat waiting for Julie's speech to begin, it really hit home. He explained to

James that we were coming to terms with not being his number one priority. All we wanted was for him to answer our phone calls and keep his promises.

"If you don't want to hang out, don't tell us you will," Derek said. "It's that simple."

"Okay, okay," James said, "I'm the worst friend ever, I'm sorry."

"Just don't let it happen again," Derek told him, even though nothing else needed to be said.

During training I was able to check the counselor list. Butthole wasn't on it. I saw him in the neighborhood throughout the school year and just recently talked to him about working as a counselor, so I could not believe he did not sign up. Butthole not being a camper was strange enough, but not having him around at all was hard to imagine. Either way, it didn't change the fact that there was work to be done. We filled out our paperwork, met with the lifeguards, and received our lunch and daily activity schedules like clockwork. The routine was the same but the faces in the room made me feel like I was working at a different park. I kept hoping to look up and hear Big White making a joke about the White Sox, but there was only the sound of shuffling papers. I imagined taking a break to visit with Becky. I'd sit down next to her and we would reminisce about growing up at The Park and argue about the home video her dad had of me doing gymnastics when I was seven. She would say, "You weren't very good." I would defend myself with, "I was trying not to show off." Instead, I stayed in my seat, reading off names and labeling emergency forms, knowing that this year the BOK dance would only be performed for memories sake.

Dale and I were in charge of the oldest boy group because Cesar started working play camp with Ashley. Most of our campers were familiar to us, so it was easy learning names. However, I no longer had all the same kids anymore. Some were now thirteen and too old to be in camp.

My work at the after school program solidified my belief that camp was about working with every kid. I did not have to continue to play favorites. Just as teachers are given a new class every fall, I had to make the most of the time I had with my campers each summer. Still I couldn't help but smile when, on the first day of camp, Butthole showed up.

I talked Julie into letting him be my counselor even though he never signed up with her. I also asked her if Frodo could complete his community service hours at The Park the same way Dale did. Because Frodo was from the neighborhood, he already knew most of the rec. leaders or references to them. Julie paired him with Nick and he took on the imaginary role of head counselor. He was young enough to be close with the counselors but old enough to drink with us at night. It was the perfect position for him, working with his friends, helping kids, and hanging out with fifteen-year-old girls.

Butthole was a good counselor, when he showed up. Two days a week he was busy with his girlfriend or skateboarding. I could tell he wanted to be off doing his own thing everyday, but it was still good for him to help out. Most of the counselors learned to be part of a worker's network without even knowing it. Showing up on time, listening to your bosses, and putting the campers before yourself were all important lessons to master. The only thing Butthole mastered was making me laugh.

Frodo turned out to be a better rec. leader/counselor than most of the paid employees we had. But one morning I saw him walking across the field about fifteen minutes late. He was not walking towards me from the direction of his house, so I assumed he stopped off somewhere before work.

I handed off the clipboard to John-Paul, "Hold this for me." I stood up and took a few steps towards Frodo. "You're late. Where you coming from, McDonald's or something?"

"No," he said. "I actually was half an hour early." He moved his head out of the sunlight and into the shade. "I got here and no one was around so I decided to walk around. I was tired so I laid down on the bench over there, behind the hill, and fell asleep."

I leaned my head in closer because I didn't think I understood, "You slept on the bench? Like a homeless guy?"

"There was a bum sleeping nearby actually," he said proudly. I gave him a look of amazement. "Well I didn't plan on falling asleep for an hour. I thought I would just close my eyes."

"Did you cover yourself in newspapers and have a bottle of vodka next to you in a brown paper bag?"

"I thought about it, but it's too hot for newspapers today."

At that moment, I was never more proud to be Frodo's friend.

When week one ended, I realized that running a group with Dale was much different than working with James or Cesar. With them, I was the newer employee, sometimes taking a backseat to their rules and ideas. Now, Dale looked at me to organize the games and control the discipline. I felt powerful. Master of the universe. We kept things simple at first, trying to get a feel for the group. While softball and hockey made appearances, most of that first week we played my creation, Ultimate Football, with the kids. This game was something we shared that no other group understood. It was our own.

July '04

A few of us went up to Wisconsin Dells for a weekend away. We were prepared for two days of camping, swimming, and relaxing. Day camp kept me grounded each summer in Chicago. Very rarely did I leave the city during the six weeks of camp, but I discovered I was missing out.

After kayaking our way down the local river early Saturday afternoon, we rented a golf cart to cruise our campsite. I was driving, with Edgar in the passenger seat and Derek and Sean in the back. We explored the multiple acres of campground for ten minutes before heading around a bank of trees and up on an open grass patch. To my surprise, a few families had set up their tents and parked their cars just around the corner. I had a choice of slamming on the brakes and hoping the cart stopped before hitting the cars, or turning back onto the road, narrowly missing a collision all together. In a split second decision, I chose the latter. Unfortunately, the golf cart did not have the same kind of traction as my Mystique, and we skidded out of control. For a moment I thought the wheels would regain traction and steer straight back for the road. Instead, the pressure of the turn flipped the cart.

Everything was blurry. Happening in a flash, yet in slow motion. *This must be a movie.* Then silence. The vehicle landed on its side in a cloud of smoke from the dirt road. My instincts told me to look at my friends, make sure they were okay. Derek and Sean were already getting out of the smashed cart. I tried to check on Edgar. He was sitting next to me, but dust was everywhere. I couldn't grasp the image in front of me. Edgar appeared to be missing, or hiding. Derek and Sean were already lying on the road, trying to gather themselves as Edgar's voice was calling out. *No, screaming.* I could see his legs now, through the dust, but not his face. His cries continued but his voice was muffled. The crash must have thrown him next to the cart. I unbuckled and used all my energy to dislodge myself from the tilted cart without tipping it. When I hit the ground I finally realized what I was hearing. Edgar was still in his seat belt, still in the passenger seat, but his body was mangled, half trapped under the tipped over cart. Derek and Sean were standing next to me, dazed for sure, but prepared to do what had to be done. Instinctually, the three of us flipped the cart over to free Edgar. Our adrenaline was so high the five hundred pound cart turned upright with ease.

Edgar's body was forced up with the cart, the seat belt connecting him to the seat. He moaned in pain as I went to unbuckle the belt. Sean was already on the phone with an ambulance. Derek and I lifted Edgar out of the seat and onto the ground.

"Don't move, we're calling an ambulance," I said in the most comforting tone I thought possible. It must have been less than a minute since the cart began to skid and yet it felt like hours of confusion had just ensued.

He was trying to talk, to tell me where the pain was the worst, but his words were rushed, his breathing short. "Hard to breathe…hurts Vince…hurts," he whispered to me, his eyes now swelling with tears.

"The ambulance is on its way," Derek said.

A few of the families camping nearby were now aware of our situation and were rushing over on their cell phones. "Is everyone okay?" a middle-aged man asked. "Did you call 911?"

"Yeah, we called already," Derek said.

"Edgar stop," Sean commanded. I looked over and Edgar was trying to stand up.

"My…back…hurts," he said. It was difficult for him to speak, his body shaking and his eyes struggling to stay open.

"I know, but stay where you are. If something is wrong, getting up could make it worse." I became overwhelmed with emotion. I feared Edgar's situation had caused a spinal injury, internal bleeding, or was life threatening. He slowly laid back on the floor and I reached out and grabbed his hand so he knew he was not alone. *Helpless*, I thought. *I am completely helpless. But so is Edgar.*

"What can we do?" Derek asked calmly. I appreciated that he was trying to be helpful as best he could rather than adding unneeded panic.

"Get my car. Here, take my keys and follow us to the hospital," I responded, trying to think of what else. "I want *you* driving."

"How long till the ambulance is here?" Sean asked.

"Soon," I told him, just now noticing the sirens in the background. "I hear it. Hurry with the car and meet back here."

Edgar was now shaking on the ground as Derek and Sean sprinted off to get my car. The ambulance arrived through the crowd of people surrounding our flipped cart. The paramedics tended to Edgar, asked questions, checked his vitals, and finally put him on a long spine board to keep his back stable. From their reactions, I feared the worst. They put him in the back of the ambulance, as Derek and Sean pulled up ready to follow.

"Who is riding with us?" a paramedic asked me.

"I am," I said. The passenger seat was comfortable, and for the first time in ten minutes I was able to breathe again. I felt somewhat optimistic: the paramedics would fix any problems, heal any wounds, cure Edgar of any injuries, and everything would be back to normal in a few hours. But, as the ambulance sped off, I kept my eyes on Edgar in back. Instead of relieving my anxieties, the first five minutes of the ride were the hardest of my life. I closed my eyes and felt a burn unlike anything I had ever felt before. Tears, dust, and blood were covering my face. *Blood? My blood?* For the first time I felt the pain on my own body. I knew I was okay though. My friend, just three feet from me on a stretcher, may not be.

The paramedics were so calm that I couldn't help but remain optimistic. Edgar was now talking to them, answering their questions, showing signs of full functionality. After what felt like an hour, but was probably only ten minutes, we arrived at the hospital.

"Go get yourself checked out," a paramedic told me. "We will run some tests on him and let you know."

I found a waiting room but they took me right in. Derek and Sean were coming in through the main entrance as I entered the examining room. "Edgar's in the back," I said, pointing to my right. I continued into the room and took a seat. The wait wasn't long for the doctor, not even enough time to wash the blood off my hands.

"Please have a seat over here," she said. "How do you feel?"

"I'm okay, mainly concerned with my friend."

"Can you take off your shirt for me?"

I removed my shirt and felt the burn of the scratches on my back. "Wow your back looks awful" she said. *Thanks doc.* "I'm going to clean it up for you. Is there anywhere else that hurts?"

I noticed the pain in my legs also. "Here," I said, pulling up my shorts. Deep scrapes that ran from my knee to my hip were swollen and littered with dry blood. *Did I get in a fight with a lion?*

"It seems like you lucked out," the doctor explained. "It could have been much worse." Despite the extreme pain I was feeling, I knew she was right.

"I know...very lucky."

"You have some deep bruising and some nasty scrapes and gashes, but nothing serious," she said. "No stitches or X-rays needed." Her words were almost bittersweet. I was truly happy nothing was wrong with me, but if Edgar was hurt bad, it would be nice to have a comparable injury to ease my guilt. "Here is a prescription for some pain medication and some extra bandages for your cuts."

"Okay, thanks," I said, reaching for the items.

"Just bring it up to the front counter and they will take care of you."

"What about my friend?"

"The doctors will talk to you in the waiting room when they know."

"Thanks again," I said as I put on my bloodied shirt and exited the door. I limped down the hallway to the waiting room, where Edgar was talking with Derek and Sean. *He's alive!*

"Hey, how are you?" I asked as I continued to approach them. At that moment my excitement was outweighing my guilt. "What did the doctors say?"

"They said I have deep back bruises and the wind was knocked out of me," Edgar responded.

In that moment, I was never more grateful. "Good," I said to him. "I'm so sorry man."

"It's okay," Edgar said. "You didn't know the cart would flip. None of us did. I do have to see a chiropractor when we get back home though. Just to make sure." His attention turned to me. "How are you? You were in there longer than I was."

"Mostly bruising, and cuts…I'll survive," I said. "You were the main concern."

The doctor came over to check on Edgar and give him a prescription. The two of us hobbled to the front desk and picked up some Vicodin and Ibuprofen. "We're all clear to go," I said to Derek across the waiting room. "As soon as you are."

"Sir? We are only here for you two," he said. "Do you want me to drive your car?"

I thought for a moment about the aches in my body but felt capable. "No thanks, I'm good."

"Let's get out of here," Edgar said, painkillers in hand.

"Shotgun!" Sean yelled out, proving life was on its way back to normal.

That last evening was rightfully somber. In the morning we packed our bags, took down our tents, and loaded up the car. Edgar, Sean, and Derek slept most of the three-hour trip home on I-90. I was left to relive the experience over and over again. (Still, to this day, I get uneasy whenever a vehicle I am in makes a sharp turn, in fear of a tip over). I dropped everyone off and was home by midday. My parents were throwing me a twentieth birthday party, but I spent most of the time resting and showing off my cuts and bruises to my family.

"Oh Vincent, please be more careful from now on," my mom said to me with a hug.

"At least I was wearing my seatbelt," I replied.

"I taught you well," she said.

"You did mom. You did."

Camp came Monday and I was still having trouble concentrating on work. All day I worried about Edgar, seeing his smashed body in my mind, hoping that there would be no long-term effects.

"Are you okay?" Caitlin asked me. "Derek told me you were in an accident."

"Actually I'm not okay," I told her, revealing my bloodied legs and the deep scrapes and bruises that lined my back, side, and chest. "My friend Edgar got it even worse."

"Oh my god, Vince," she said covering her mouth in shock. "This is awful."

"Not as awful as going through it," I said.

"I'm glad you're okay," she said giving me a hug.

I'm a little better now...

Crayons, markers, and colored pencils were flying all around the room. Another failed art project for my group. The oldest boys hated art, they have since I was in camp, and they probably always will. Caitlin ducked away from a flying jungle-green and ran over to me.

I admired the way she always put on a genuine smile when she saw me. I had known her since my first year working at The Park and she seemed like she always belonged. "Hey, what's up?"

"I'm looking for some markers so my girls can color these posters upstairs," she said looking at my out of control boys.

I grabbed the marker bucket my boys were using and motioned to her with it. "Here, we just finished using these." She came over and took the bucket from my hand. "What did you do on your birthday?" Her seventeenth birthday, which was yesterday, had come the day after my twentieth.

"Ate cheesecake and cried because my dad didn't show up for dinner." She clarified for me, "He's an ass."

"I'll take you out tonight to make up for it," I told her. Red-Orange just hit Gabe in the head. I looked at Caitlin, "Sorry, I have to take care of this." I walked over to the table of boys who were throwing the Crayolas. Caitlin went back up the stairs to her group. It was at this point two years ago where I would have went ballistic and started yelling, but almost nothing phased me anymore. "Looks like you guys want to sit on the side of the pool for the first half of swim today."

"Swimming sucks anyway," Carlos said.

"Fine, it's up to you guys. Clean up the mess and swim, or sit on the side of the pool."

They mumbled to each other and started picking up their mess. "Can we go play football?" Carlos asked. "Art sucks."

"Sure," I said. "Once this place is clean."

By the end of the day I had forgot all about my comment to Caitlin. I drove to work now because I was too lazy to make the one and a half mile walk in the morning, so I was headed to my car when I heard her yell, "Vince!"

"Yes Caitlin," I mocked. "How can I help you my dear?"

She gave me a look that meant I was either stupid or not funny. Perhaps both. "So what's the plan for tonight?"

I spun my memory Rolodex to remember why 'tonight' was significant. It finally stopped on her dad's face in a piece of cheesecake. "We can go to the movies. I know *Anchorman* and *The Notebook* are playing, if you're interested."

She said, "Okay, I'll look up times and call you to decide when we want to go."

"Sounds like a plan," I said. "I'm going to go take a nap so don't call me before six."

"Haha, okay. Me too, I'm tired as hell. Bye."

"Bye."

I pulled the car out of the parking lot and turned onto Irving Park Road. It was about six lights to my house and I seemed to make every one. There was no one parked on my side of the block so I pulled up in front and cut the ignition. *Today's a good day.* I went inside my house and headed into the kitchen where I turned on the Sox game. I searched for some food to calm my hunger and settled on a Snickers bar and a glass of lemonade. *Delicious.* The sports section of the newspaper was on the table so I flipped through it as I downed my snack. I wanted to fight off sleep long enough to watch the end of the game, but I knew I needed the rest. The door to my room was open and I saw my bed waiting for me. Three forty-five shined from my alarm clock. I set my alarm for six and passed out within two minutes.

I dreamt about going to the mall with Keith and buying a snowboard. A moment later we were walking to his car and hopped in. Cars were moving so fast around us that we were unable to maneuver through the parking garage. I heard a siren going off. *Maybe that is why everyone is in a rush.* I never got a chance to find out because I woke up.

The alarm was beeping at a high frequency. I could feel that my cheek was drenched with drool. *How is this possible?* The clock read six o'clock. *Two hours gone by already?* I checked my phone and had no missed calls. Hot water from the shower was calling, so I decided to jump in and wake myself up. As I finished washing my hair I heard my ring tone. The knob was cold as I turned off the water, reached for the nearest towel, and jumped out of the fiberglass tub.

"Did I wake you?" the voice on the other line inquired.

"No, I just got out of the shower." I assumed it was Caitlin on the phone, but the number was unfamiliar to me.

"Well *Anchorman* is playing at seven thirty at Crown if you still want to go." Now I recognized her voice. "Or there is *The Notebook* at eight ten."

"I'd prefer Anchorman," I said with my shoulder keeping the phone up to my ear. My hands were busy drying me off. "Is that good with you? I can pick you up at seven."

"Okay. Call me when you are in front of my house."

"Will do." I hung up the phone and finished drying off. I found a pair of khaki shorts and a nice shirt and went downstairs to eat something. My mom was making grilled cheese and soup. Simple and satisfying. I went online to check some baseball scores until the food was done and sat down with my family to eat.

"You look nice," my sister Mercedes said to me. "Hot date?"

"Just going out with Caitlin. Going to see *Anchorman*."

"Oh, it's really funny. I think you'll like it."

"That's what everyone keeps saying." I devoured a sandwich and poured some crackers into my soup. I ate quickly and loaded my bowl and spoon into the dishwasher. Before I headed out the door, I brushed my teeth and used some mouthwash. *Mint green.*

I called Caitlin when I was outside her house, "I'm here."

"I'll be right down," she said.

I wondered if she thought it was a real date. *Caitlin's great...really great, but she's not even in college and I'm entering my third year in the fall.* I knew it couldn't work so I never really thought about it. She closed and locked her front door and began to walk towards my car. *She looks hot.*

"Hey there."

"Hi. You look nice," I said honestly. Her long blonde hair was straight out of a Pantene Pro V commercial. Her perfect red lips added to her great smile. I was still wondering what she expected out of this night as we drove away. "Did you nap after camp?"

"Yeah, I called you as soon as I woke up. I set my alarm for six but I must have hit the snooze." I felt more comfortable talking with her than I did with any of my previous girlfriends. "Do you want to split some popcorn when we get there?" she asked.

"Yeah, sounds good." I turned onto the highway and started to pick up speed. "You can look at my CDs. See if there are any you like." She reached for my CD book and began flipping through the pages. I was glad to have just bought Boyz II Men's greatest hits, it rounded out my collection. It is always good to have a couple old time slow jams mixed in with your Blink 182 and Green Day.

"Is this your CD?" she asked with a giggle.

I glanced over and saw her pointing to my Boyz II Men. "Haha no, probably my sister's," I lied. *Damn you Motown-philly!* "I guess you can put that in if you *really* want."

"No, that's okay. I got one, don't look," she said. I kept my eyes on the road as she slid a CD into the player. Jimmy Eat World's *Bleed American* came on. "This is my favorite CD."

I looked over at her closing the CD case. "It's a good one," is all I could think to say. I began to run a monologue in my head. *Why are conversations so much harder when there is the pressure of a date? This wasn't even a date anyway. Just two friends seeing a movie. I probably could make out with her if I wanted. No, that would be too weird. But so good. She has been chasing after me for three years now. I bet she's a good kisser.*

I snapped out of it when she skipped songs on the CD. "Best song ever," she said. "It's called *Hear You Me*."

"Oh I know," I told her honestly.

"So, how are all your cuts and bruises from the crash?" she asked.

It had been less than a week since the accident, but most of the cuts had healed. "I'm getting back to one hundred percent," I answered. "Just the bruises on my back and thigh. The cuts are pretty much healed."

"Well that's good news."

"It is." Our exit was next so I merged over to get off. "I hope the movie isn't sold out."

"I didn't even think of that," she said. "We'll be okay."

Despite the theater being filled with hundreds of Will Ferrell fans, we found seats. We sat arm to arm the entire movie. *A sign perhaps?* I continuously contemplated making a move but froze. Every joke or obscene part of the movie seemed to lighten the tension and leave me time to act, but I wanted to make sure I wasn't going to make a move just for the kiss. I had had too many relationships based on temporary feelings and I knew Caitlin and I could never be a fling. I wanted to be sure of what I was getting myself into.

The movie ended and we rose from our seats. In the lobby I noticed there was no ticket vendors on duty. "Do you want to see *The Notebook* too?" I asked her.

"Yeah," she answered without hesitation. Like she was waiting for me to ask.

Without drawing attention to our plan, we snuck into the theater showing *The Notebook*, found seats in the middle of the theater, and sat down. I hoped this movie would keep me awake. I thought Caitlin might be thinking the same thing, "Are you tired?"

She looked up at me like I was crazy. "No, are you?"

I didn't want to disappoint. "I'm fine, I just wanted to make sure you didn't pass out ten minutes into it." A new set of previews began to roll.

I noticed Caitlin inching closer towards me in her seat, *or was it just the power of The Notebook?* The last time I was this nervous around a girl I was a freshman in high school. It didn't make sense. She leaned her arm against mine, *what do I do?* Did she want me to make a move? Did she just want to be comfortable? Fucking Shit. No time, the movie began.

I don't know if you have ever seen *The Notebook*. If you haven't, you should. It is hard to explain the power that movie can have over you. I decided that night that I would marry Caitlin and build her a house.

Too bad I was too scared to tell her that. I dropped her off at two A.M. without telling her how I felt. It didn't matter though. We were going to spend everyday together for the rest of our lives.

A week later, Caitlin and I had our first kiss. We spent everyday together at work and every night together after camp. On the weekends, we would hang out at my house until her curfew. Then we would hop into my car and I would drive her home. An hour or so later, once her parents were asleep, she would sneak out and find me back in front of her house, ready to spend a few more hours together. The two of us would lay on my living room floor, watching movies and eating popcorn, hoping time would just stop so life could be this way forever. We never wanted to be apart. We didn't know *how* to be apart.

James loved chicken fights on the wrestling mat. The object was to stand on one leg and hop around while trying to knock over your opponent. If they fell, put two feet on the ground, or were pushed off the mat, the match was over.

J.P., who resembled Paul Bunyan, was about five feet and two hundred pounds as a twelve year old in my group. He was not a blob-like two hundred pounds, but a solid block of mass. Carlos was the same build as J.P., just twenty pounds lighter and slightly more agile. They were the kings of chicken fighting.

James would bring his campers to the auditorium while Dale and I had our group in there. Most of the campers were at one point or another in his group, so he knew all the potentially entertaining match ups. He enjoyed putting Carlos and J.P. on the same team and watching them destroy normal-sized children.

Chicken fights were a nice change of pace for our groups. Too often we played outside in the heat all day and kids would get tired before lunch. The auditorium was air conditioned and provided a much-needed cool down. We even agreed to share time with Veronica's group when the heat index topped one hundred. Her girls would show almost no interest in the intense matches taking place, providing only a glance or occasional moan when someone hit the floor hard.

We were usually good about creating matches so that everyone would participate. Sometimes we would have three little guys team up against Butthole, put Dale, James, and me against our seven or so counselors, or just have a royal rumble where everyone got to jump onto the large green mat. Because there were so many people involved in the free-for-all, the winner was usually someone unexpected. Two friends would knock out J.P. while Carlos would get pushed off by a ten year old he didn't see. The final two survivors could easily be seventy pound Gabe versus unathletic Hershel. The winner would be king for the rest of the day, earning respect he never thought possible. Everyone else would be looking forward to revenge the next time we unrolled the giant green mat.

And so it was, summer moved along too quickly for my liking. Katie was forced to take over art room duty instead of having a group of her own, so Dale and I cut a deal with her: we would attend art and she would not force our boys to do the art projects everyone else was doing. She agreed without hesitation. Ashley, who normally just ran play camp, became the office junky, spending every hour outside of play camp sitting behind Gene's desk. By the end of July, Frodo had finished his service hours but still worked for free a few days a week. I was growing so accustomed to having him around that camp felt different on days when he didn't show.

As for Caitlin and I, we kept our relationship out of the workplace. Most people didn't even know we were together, which led to some interesting conversations.

"Do you want to hang out tonight?" Veronica asked me after a typical camp day. "Maybe get some dinner and catch up on things…I feel like I haven't talk to you in a while."

"Well, I'm busy tonight actually. Caitlin and I are going to hang out with some of her friends."

"You seem to be hanging out with her a lot. What's that all about?"

"We're going out," I said.

Her facial reaction was complete shock. "Really, since when?"

"About a week now," I told her. "It all happened very sudden and we haven't been telling people because we don't know where it will lead."

"That's weird, Ashley was just telling me that she thought the two of you might be together, but I figured there's no way I couldn't know."

"Yeah, well, I'm a bad friend," I said, truly sorry for making the situation awkward.

"Okay, well if you two are ever *not* hanging out, let me know."

"Will do."

It wasn't just Veronica who was confused by the whole situation. Some of the guys gave me grief over the time I was spending with Caitlin. I quickly thought about James and Joanne and decided that Caitlin would understand that I wanted time with my friends. Plus Julie warned that we could get fired if we were caught making out.

August '04

Katie was on her last week of work at The Park. I assumed she did not want to spend her future summers off from teaching working at camp. She wanted to retire with a bang, but didn't want to just have another traditional party. I made a suggestion.

Dale once had a birthday party at a place called Whirly-Ball. Katie agreed that it would be a fitting coworker outing, as long as we drank some beer afterwards.

WhirlyBall can be a violent game. Two teams battle it out by driving bumper cars around a rink trying to shoot a whiffle ball into a net. The ball is passed from player to player by use of an eighteen-inch plastic scoop. When you play with friends, all rules and regulations get thrown out the window. The cars become battering rams and the scoops become prehistoric clubs.

The referee was going over the rules with our group as I looked around at the faces of those present. Still no Katie. I wondered how she could request a night out and not show up herself.

"Where is this girl?" Cesar asked. "I thought it was her big send off."

"Yeah, her retirement party," I said. "I left her two messages already. Maybe she fell asleep."

Cesar hopped into a red car and tightened his seat belt. "She'll show."

"I hope so," I said as I got comfortable in my yellow car.

Frodo, Dale, Nick and myself had the advantage of playing before. We played on the same team the first game and won two to zero. It would have been easier to score if we followed the rule of 'no bumping from behind.' It also would have been easier on the thighs and back if we played within the rules. After six ten-minute games, most of us were having trouble walking. Even with the pain, the fun of that night started another park tradition.

Katie never did show, so our plans for after WhirlyBall fell apart. On the car ride home I thought about how her priorities have changed since my first few summers. She was always the first one at the parties and the last one to leave. Now she was too busy to even remember her own going away party. Camp must have lost its meaning to Katie and had become just another job.

At the morning meeting Katie apologized for falling asleep on us. Napping was extremely typical when you worked at a summer camp, so we all understood. Still, we talked about the night before as Jaimie showed off her bruises. WhirlyBall had gotten the best of us, but she was the worst. Her body was so badly bruised it looked like she fell down a flight of stairs.

The last two days of camp came and went in a flash. Gene talked again about retiring but scratched the idea shortly after. Dale was tempted to grow his hair back out to regain 'dreamboat status,' but chose to retain the John Elway look instead. Nick continued his run of talent show performances involving line dancing, this time with the "Cha Cha Slide." Grace, my savior when it came to straightening out Gabe, saved me again. This time it was last second costume changes for our talent show. She helped dress our lone female role, her brother, in an old dress of hers. His red skirt didn't falter one inch as he seduced the crowd to his favorite tune, "Like a Virgin." And, after six years, Katie said goodbye to The Park.

Gene offered Nick a year-round position when camp ended. He was one of the few rec. leaders who stayed in Chicago for school, and the opportunity was a perfect match for him. With the new job, Nick still got to spend time with Gene and Julie year round, work with kids, and set up sporting events. I envied him.

Again, I packed up my life and loaded up my car for another year of college. I had been accepted into the College of Education and was about to begin my core classes for my junior year. People at school discussed how lesson plans and integrated units were going to consume every minute of free time I had for my last two years. *I'm so happy.*

I stopped by Caitlin's house before I went down to school, to spend my last few hours in Chicago with her. I began to feel that I was making a huge mistake by leaving. It was ten in the morning when I rang her doorbell. She came down her steps, opened the door, and led me up into her apartment. Her parents weren't home so we had the house to ourselves. Usually we were confined to her room but we laid down on the living room floor and put in *The Nightmare Before Christmas*, her favorite movie. I held her close and dozed a bit here and there, only waking when Jack the Pumpkin King would break into song.

"Hey Vince," I woke up startled.

"Yeah," my voice was scratchy and my eyes were still closed.

I could feel Caitlin rolling over next to me. "Shouldn't your mom be coming soon?" she asked.

I opened my eyes and felt for my phone. "Yeah, in about two minutes," I said, suddenly realizing that I had slept away my last few hours with Caitlin. "I don't want to leave."

"Then don't," she said, making it sound so easy. "If you stay, it will be summer forever."

"That would be alright with me," I said, sitting up and wiping the sleep from my eyes. I put my keys and wallet back into my pockets and reached for my phone. It rang before I could touch it.

"No, don't answer it," Caitlin pleaded. "Don't go."

"I have to, you know I do." I answered the phone and told my mom I would be right down. Caitlin opened her door and walked me to the bottom of the stairs. "Being with you is so simple," I said to her, trying to say exactly what I felt. "This is good, really good."

"When will I see you again?" she asked as tears began to fall down her cheek.

"Soon." I hugged her and held her in my arms until I knew it was time to go. "I'll call you when I get settled in."

"Bye Vince."

"Bye Caitlin."

I left with our relationship status uncertain. I knew I wanted to be with her, but realistically, I was unsure if the distance would be too much to overcome. As I drove down to school I couldn't help but think that my life as I knew it was over. Caitlin was going to find someone else at school. I was going to flunk out of college because I had no idea what integrated units were. Not even the after school program could save me. Because my class schedule did not allow me to work everyday, my boss declined my reenrollment. I was again going to be living with Edgar, but with two new roommates as well. I had no idea if I was going to end up fighting with them too. My life was in shambles and the one thing that always made sense to me was ten months away.

My mom and I talked the entire drive down to Champaign. Our conversation touched on everything from school, to Caitlin, to music. Still I could not help but feel that this drive was the biggest mistake of my life.

"I hate school!" I yelled as we entered the cornfields of Central Illinois.

Year Five

With registration time approaching, I made an appointment to see my advisor to go over my schedule for the spring semester. As I waited outside her door I glanced over the packet of information she gave me last time. She had told me to go home and plan out my final three semesters and any summer school I may have needed. I browsed the university class list for hours upon hours, trying to find classes that would allow me to graduate on time. Finally I held in my hands what I thought was the perfect schedule.

"Come in Vince," my advisor, Kathy, spoke from in her office. I grabbed my paperwork and proceeded down the hall to her cubicle. "Have a seat please. I was just looking over your scheduling and I'm wondering if you were planning on taking an extra semester after student teaching."

"Um, no I wasn't. I mapped out my schedule and as long as I get the classes, I can be done in May of '06." She looked back at her monitor and I began to get nervous. Maybe I overlooked something or took a class I wasn't supposed to. "Here." I handed her my filled out schedule. "This is what I came up with."

She took the schedule and grimaced slightly. I knew she didn't want to disappoint me, but I wanted the truth. Then she said, "There are a few problems with this schedule." Game over.

"Oh...like what?" I asked sincerely.

"First things first," she started. "You cannot take electives senior year. You are only allowed to take your final education courses and your two student teaching clincals." Apparently I was supposed to just know this. "The guidelines are listed on the education website." *Oh.* "Also, if you try to take all of your final electives over this summer, it will be nearly impossible to get into all of them." She was tallying up all of the classes I still needed to take. "Yeah, it would be six classes this summer. The maximum is three, maybe four if you get it approved, but you cannot take six classes in one summer."

I was becoming more frustrated than ever. I had already been taking extra classes every semester plus summer school to make sure I could graduate on time. Now I still fell short.

"What if I take extra classes this spring? Then this summer I will only have four summer classes. I know it will be twenty hours or more but I can't stay here another semester."

"Listen Vince," Kathy interrupted, "you are already full for the spring, seven classes. You're best off just taking three classes this summer and three the summer after you student teach. Then you can still participate in the May ceremony."

This new bit of information left a small glimmer of hope. "I can still walk in May with my friends?"

"Yes. We allow you to walk in spring if you are finishing in summer. As long as you are enrolled in all the classes you need to graduate, you will be fine." Kathy, my savior.

"Can I take those last three summer classes back in Chicago?"

"It looks like you already took classes away from U of I," she pointed out.

"Yeah, last summer."

"You have to complete your first three years here in order to finish up somewhere else." She continued explaining,

"You could finish in Chicago but you could not earn your diploma from us." That was out of the question.

I said, "Okay, well I will make it work. I'll let you know when I register for the summer to make sure I am on track." I rose from my seat.

"Bye Vince, have a good break."

"Thanks Kathy, you too."

I strolled out of her office and exited the Education Building with mixed emotions. I thought I was all set before I went in, but considering how bad the situation could have been, staying in Champaign another semester, paying more rent, and being without my friends, I ended up okay. Just two more years of summer school. Class was never as bad when you only have three at a time. Things were going to be okay. Then it hit me as I was walking into my apartment. I wouldn't be able to work at The Park during the summer of 2006. There was no way camp and class overlap wouldn't overlap. I contemplated the situation many times, but each time with the same result. Next summer was going to be my last at The Park.

Immediately I thought about Caitlin. We were still together and were managing fairly well despite the distance and age obstacles. I went home nearly every weekend to see her, via a Greyhound bus or Edgar's black Mustang. The travel was hectic and overwhelming at times, but I never thought about staying at school and not seeing her. I fumbled through my pockets for my cell phone to call Caitlin and tell her the bad news.

April '05

I came home the same weekend every spring to take my drug test for camp. This was going to be the first time since last summer that most of the rec. leaders would see each other again. After class on Friday I made a quick stop home, gathered my belongings, and walked over to the Greyhound station. I found a seat towards the front of the bus. I always hoped that the seat next to me would remain vacant. I watched with my head against the glass window as the passengers, college students and Champaign residents, came aboard. Each person passed and no one sat next to me. *Maybe I smell.* I was glad I didn't shower before I left. The bus took off and I stretched my legs across the empty seat. I opened up my backpack and reached for my book, *Harry Potter and the Order of the Phoenix*. I had only started reading the series because it was the thing to do if you were under the age of thirty. Now I couldn't stop. Either way, it was going to keep me occupied for the next three hours.

I woke up with the book in my hand and the Chicago skyline in view. Caitlin picked me up and we went back to my house to eat dinner with my parents. It used to be a big deal coming home from school, but now, because of Caitlin, I was accustomed to seeing my family every weekend. My dad talked about the fast start the White Sox were having to the baseball season.

"We're looking good, definitely," I replied, "but we always seem to fall apart in the second half." I put another spoon full of rice onto my plate and asked Caitlin if she wanted some as well. She told me she was full and went back to sipping on her glass of Orange Sunkist.

"So how do you like the classroom you're in?" my mom asked me.

I was observing a fourth grade classroom for one of my education classes. "Well I have to take the bus for fifteen minutes, then get off and walk, every time I go," I complained. The school was in Urbana, the city that housed half of my university, but I was a Champaign guy. "It's kinda B.S. if the buses don't even go all the way out to the school."

"They could have put you farther away though," Caitlin reminded me.

"Yeah, you're right," I said truthfully, thinking of some friends who were observing forty minutes away. "I mean it's good. My teacher likes to tell me a lot of personal things though. About himself and some of the other teachers. Like he told me how he had a party for all the teachers and which ones were really drunk and out of control."

"He probably shouldn't be saying that kind of stuff to you," my mom stated.

"I know, I think it's because I'm a young guy and he wants to seem cool."

She gave a look of disappointment that was directed at him, "Well his job is to help you get a feel for the classroom…not to make you think he's cool."

"I know that. Don't be mad at me," I said.

"You call this mad?" she asked, now appearing *actually* angry.

"Forget it. Really he is a good teacher. He lets me basically tutor the kids, but I haven't taught a lesson yet."

"If he lets you teach, you should jump at the opportunity," my dad added.

"I know, I will," I promised.

Caitlin was already finished eating, so I devoured the rest of my food and the two of us went downstairs. My basement was like my own apartment. I spent most of my time down there because my parents helped me fix it up into a nice living area, kitchen, and bathroom. That night Caitlin and I discussed moving my bedroom into the basement as well. The cold and loneliness of it would be offset by the privacy and chance to really feel like I had my own place. We sat up talking about how I would have my bed and furniture arranged as *Seinfeld* reruns played in the background.   "It's time for me to go," Caitlin whispered in my ear.

I opened my blurry eyes to check the clock. Nearly two in the morning. Once graduation came Caitlin would not have a curfew, but for the next two months it was two A.M. "Okay babe." I stood up and walked with her to my back door. "Do you have everything?"

"Yeah," she nodded.

"Thanks for picking me up today," I gave her a hug. "I love you, good night."

She kissed me, "I love you too. Call me in the morning. Good night."

I closed the door behind her and turned off the basement lights. I was tired from my long day so I went straight to bed when she left. As I laid half asleep I thought about how much she meant to me. We had not even been dating one year and I could not see my life without her. When it came to teaching, she was my biggest supporter. I knew that no matter how daunting student teaching and having my own classroom would be, she would be there to encourage me. Plus, she picked me up every Friday night from the Greyhound station, even though she is scared of highway driving and getting lost. I decided I must have won her in some lottery. But fuck it, you know what they say, 'sometimes it is better to be lucky than good.' I also finally understood how James must have felt about Joanne. He never really saw the situation as him choosing her over us; in his eyes, he didn't have a choice. He had to be with her. I knew how he felt. I fell asleep thinking about last school year and how I could have approached things differently with James and Joanne.

I awoke to my cell phone ringing. It was my cousin, Julia. She was sixteen and had recently been hired to work at The Park. "Hey Vince, did I wake you?"

"I have to get up anyway, what's up?" I yawned and wiped the sleep away from my eyes.

"I wanted to know if you can pick me up for the drug test today."

"Oh, yeah that's not a problem. I'm leaving my house in about an hour."

"Okay, I'll be ready. Is there anything I need to bring?" Ah, first year jitters.

"Just a full bladder."

"Okay, then call me when you're here."

"Sounds good."

I picked up Julia and then Caitlin that Saturday morning. I also called Dale when we were almost to Warren Park. He was already in line. I opened the front doors and saw the massive line of people waiting to pee in cups. We walked to the end and saw Dale standing there, looking nervous.

"Hey guys, are you ready for this?" he said like it was a calculus final.

"I'm ready to go," Caitlin responded. She took her place in line against the wall. I followed behind her.

"I have to piss like a racehorse," I said. "I hope I don't get a bladder infection." I looked at some of the faces in line in front of us, trying to see anyone from our park. Then I remembered last year and how Dale pissed right before he came so he had to spend half the day in line drinking water in order to go. I looked at him and asked, "Are *you* ready this year?"

"Haha, I think so. I have to poo also. Real bad." Maybe that was why he had a concerned look earlier.

"That's gross Dale," Caitlin commented.

"Well I do," he said emphatically. "What about you Julia, are you excited for your first pee test?"

"So excited Bobby!" *Who the hell is Bobby?*

"I have no idea what you just said to me," Dale aimed his confusion at Julia. "Did you call me Bobby?"

"Yes I said Bobby, but you're not Bobby. I just say that man, like all the time, it's my thing." She was gloating over a rather weird habit.

The four of us looked ahead and saw Jaimie and Grace enter the building. Grace mouthed something to Jaimie when she saw the length of the line. "Fuck" probably. They walked towards us to join the end.

"Hey losers," Dale said to them, getting their attention.

"Oh, I didn't even see you guys," Jaimie said. "How long have you been here?"

"Only two minutes," Dale said, "but the line has been moving pretty fast actually."

Grace looked from Dale, to Julia, to me. "Oh yeah. Grace, Jaimie, this is my cousin Julia. She's working camp with us." Julia gave them a casual wave and smile.

"Hi Julia," Jaimie said, keeping her eyes out for recently arriving people who she would have to beat to the end of the line. "I didn't know if you would be back this year old man," she said to me when she realized the coast was clear.

"Wow! Nice to see you too," I said smiling and shaking my head.

"Come on," Jaimie said to Grace grabbing her arm. They smiled at us and walked to the end of the line, which was now ten people behind us.

"They didn't even say 'hi' to me," Caitlin said stating a fact rather than complaining.

"That's because they hate you," Dale said in an inconspicuous tone.

"They probably do," she replied. "Eh, whatever."

"Have they worked at The Park for long?" Julia asked.

"A couple years," Caitlin answered her inquiring mind. "Jaimie is so frustrating at times."

"Why is that?" Dale asked.

Caitlin turned her fiery gaze at Dale, "Are you serious? Because all she does is flirt with you and Derek at work." Dale shrugged his shoulders like he was oblivious to this piece of information. "Don't even give me that Dale, you know she does. And, Jaimie knows you have a girlfriend, so that makes things even worse."

As Dale and Caitlin continued their disagreement over Jaimie's actions, I explained to Julia my take on the situation. How Jaimie often flirted with Dale at camp but that she was single and allowed to flirt all she wanted. Nevertheless, it was not my concern.

We chatted in line for twenty more minutes about school, camp, and our families. Dale had a new shouting match with his sister to talk about, and Caitlin, another fight with her parents. My problems were with my roommates at school. I was sick of seeing dishes overflowing in the sink. They all denied that the mess was theirs because it was easier to point the finger at someone else when living in a four-bedroom apartment. We also had an eviction notice on our door every couple of weeks because one roommate never paid rent on time. Julia tried to soak in all of this information, which Dale and Caitlin heard from me on a regular basis.

"Sometimes he wouldn't pay for months," I explained, trying to stay calm. "When he claimed he paid all of his rent but we still were receiving letters from our landlord, I went to check it out personally. The landlord pulled out our file and receipts to show me that we were thousands of dollars behind in rent. Apparently he was paying rent for only half of the months." I turned to Dale and Caitlin, both high school seniors preparing for a possible future of college roommates. "If you want to end a friendship in a hurry, live with someone who screws you over with rent."

"Sounds like you're enjoying school this year," Dale said sympathetically.

"Oh yeah, it's a blast."

By the time we reached the front of the line my bladder was about to erupt. Caitlin was the first to be called to fill her cup.

"Good luck Bobby!"

Caitlin kept walking to the bathroom but could be seen shaking her head in disapproval of the message. I'm glad I wasn't a girl during the test. I don't know how they aim their stream into that cup. Maybe they had special training.

I was called up next and took my cup inside the stall. I filled the cup and had to finish off in the toilet. Most people walked out with half a cup at most, I could have had a pint. *I should enter a competition.* I walked out, gave my sample to the waiting nurse, and saw Dale walking in after me. "Good luck my young apprentice," I joked with him.

"I will try Master," he said back.

I spotted Julia behind Dale, still waiting for her turn. "You look nervous."

"I am! What if I can't go?"

"Just relax and take your time, even if it feels like it's taking ten minutes. Better to go in ten minutes that come out with an empty cup."

"Okay Bobby, thanks." Julia was called in a second later and I continued out into the hallway.

"Where's Dale?" Caitlin asked.

"Still in there. I went in before him," I said.

"Oh. I don't know if I filled up my cup enough. The lady said it was probably just enough to test," she said, putting her hair up in a ponytail. "Where is everyone else?"

I looked for anyone I might know in line as Caitlin leaned her head against my chest. "Derek won't test till summer and everyone else must be coming later," I answered. I put my arm around Caitlin and whispered "I love you" into her ear. She looked up at me and kissed me on the cheek. *Today's a good day.* We stood there waiting for another minute in our own world.

Julia was first out and I saw a look of relief on her face. "Oh my God Bobby, I did it!" she said so that nearly everyone in line could hear. "Still no Dale?" she asked, shrugging off the onlookers.

"Actually, speak of the devil," I said. Dale was walking out of the bathroom towards us. He had a giant smile on his face. "Sir, what took so long?"

"I'll tell you outside," he said. We left the park house and started walking towards our cars. "So, remember how I had to take a shit?" He started to laugh at his own words. "Well, I couldn't fill my cup without letting it all out, so I had to do both."

It was taking a second to process his words. "Wait," I said. "Everyone else is pissing in the stalls and worried about filling up their cups and you're sitting back on the toilet, taking a dump?" I was amazed. "You're my hero."

"Sheebs. I had no choice man, when you gotta go, you gotta go."

"You never stop surprising me," Caitlin said, patting Dale on the back.

"Thanks," Dale responded smiling. "Alright, I'll call you guys later." He got into his car as we kept walking to mine.

"This year is off to a good start," I remarked to Caitlin. "Fuckin' Dale."

"So what are you guys doing now?" Julia asked us while I fit the key into my door. I looked at Caitlin who seemed to know what was on my mind.

"Going to get Taco Bell for lunch. You want some?" I asked her.

"Taco Bell? No thanks, Bobby!"

"Your loss," Caitlin said. That it was.

I spent the rest of the weekend with Caitlin. April was the first month in Chicago where there were signs of summer. It was not uncommon to start out with a snow or hail storm and end with kids playing outside in shorts. The weather was somewhere in between that weekend.

On Sunday night Caitlin told me that her parents were considering remodeling the basement of their brick two-flat apartment building. Once finished, Caitlin and her older sister Nicole would move in. For years her parents had contemplated giving them their own place, but talks would fizzle just as quickly as they began. Now they appeared more serious, actually looking into contractors and getting price quotes. I was eager because a new apartment meant Caitlin and I would not be confined to the bedroom she shared with her younger sister. I also loved the idea of my younger girlfriend graduating from high school and moving into her own place. Just yesterday it felt like she was a thirteen-year-old counselor chasing me around all summer, and now she would soon be a college chick with her own apartment. How time flies.

While planning of the apartment was underway, I had to head back to school. It was just after dawn on Monday, the sun was rising over Lake Michigan and peeking through the skyline, as my dad and I drove east on the Kennedy Expressway. He dropped me off at the Greyhound station. "Here, some spending money," he said, handing me a couple of twenties. My dad always knew when to help me out and when to let me be on my own. Holding back tears, I gave him a hug before getting out of the car.

"I'll see you next weekend," I told him. I felt so lucky at that moment, to be in the situations I was in, with Caitlin, my friends, and my parents. Then I thought of my roommates and realized my life wasn't perfect after all. When I opened the terminal door I spotted my bus already boarding. I jumped in line at the end, handed my ticket to the driver, and sat in the back. I placed my bag on the seat next to me, pulled out my CD player with Green Day's *American Idiot* inside, put the headphones to my ears, and drifted away. The morning ride always went by quickly. The bus was nearly empty and I always suffered from sleep deprivation from my weekends with Caitlin.

At times, I thought about the upcoming summer. My last year at camp, last chance to talk baseball with Cesar, one more summer with my campers, but most importantly, three months non-stop with Caitlin.

She had become everything to me and everyone else was being pushed down the totem pole. When I came home from school every weekend, we worked on our relationship and how to cope with the long distance. It was hard setting aside friends we had for years, but we knew that in order to stay together, we needed to spend what little time we had together being in our own world.

Only two weeks left of school my junior year. It was surreal to think about it all.

June '05

Summer came in a heartbeat as the cool May weather finally subsided and gave way to a blistering June. The smell of summer was in the air. Perhaps too hot during the midday, it was the perfect temperature to spend the evenings outside. But I was spending most of my nights reading. Reading was never an important part of my life, even as an aspiring teacher. Even though I managed to read *The Lord of the Rings* freshman year of college, I avoided reading most of my assigned books for classes. I just figured there were better ways to entertain myself. Then, I found myself unable to put down J.K. Rowling's *Harry Potter* series at the end of my junior year. Fantasy stories were forever my thing and I was just now learning the power of reading versus watching them. I longed for the next book in the series. Would Harry die in the end? Were Hermoine and Ron ever going to hook up? Is Snape really a good guy or just a helluva liar? Endless questions. But nothing more than a young man's inner child finding interest in dragons and magic. And then, when summer began, I finished *The Order of the Phoenix*.

More. I needed more.

The next book in the *Potter* series would come out that summer, but I couldn't wait. I was tempted to read the series over again. Start the first book the day I finished the fifth. I temporarily filled my hunger with all seven books in *The Chronicles of Narnia*, but I finished those in two weeks. It was middle school level reading, child's play to any college student. I needed something more.

My previous semester I had an English class that went over how to approach teaching literacy in our own classrooms.

While organization and imagination were topics often discussed, the most important was filling your life with books. "Go out and read as many books as you can," my professor would say. "Kids' books, action books, romance books, adult books, books of poetry, short stories, even the newspaper. Read it all."

So I did.

I felt like Darth Vader, kneeling over in front of my English professor during her speech on reading. "Yes master," I said with my head down, "I will read as many books as I can. There will be no one to stop us this time."

I *wanted* to read, for one of the few times in my life. My mom recommended books for me to tackle next. Books written by people my age, *Small Town Odds* and *Twelve*, were up first. Novels by Dan Brown, *The Da Vinci Code* and *Angels and Demons*, were next. Soon I had my own taste in writing style. I was reading a book a week, sometimes two. Caitlin began reading as well. Her final high school novel was Mario Puzo's *The Godfather*, and she couldn't put it down. I craved wizards and witches. She craved sex, drugs, and killing. She even threatened me once that I would be "sleeping with the fishes," unless I agreed to rent the movie of her choice.

Two weeks before camp started I was perusing the selection at Barnes and Nobles for more summer reading. I preordered *Harry Potter and the Half Blood Prince*, the next in the series, but was no longer limited to enjoying fantasy novels. I searched several sections looking for books, filling my hands with so many that my fingers were strained trying to hold them all. It was quite the adjustment for me to spend over a hundred dollars on a dozen books when I had previously never spent that much on books in my entire life.

I unpacked the paperbacks from their bags when I got home. Already their appearance made me feel more like a teacher than I had before. With camp starting soon I decided it would be best to read a few books my campers might be familiar with. *Just one more way to find common ground*, I thought to myself.

Summer school was the only thing stopping me from devouring three books a week. I couldn't get into all the classes I needed, but I was still taking two general education courses. They were short, running about half the length of a fall or spring semester course, so the workload came at me twice as fast. Still, I held out hope that I could beat the system and work at The Park next year.

Amidst my summer reading and homework, I stopped by The Park to see the list of summer employees. Julia's name was now present, but not seeing Nick, Katie, or Veronica's names brought a sense of sadness. I had known since last summer that they would not be rec. leaders, but only then did I realize how much the list had changed since my first year. Usually I kept in touch with former employees, but this last school year I tried to concentrate on my family, Caitlin, and my close guy friends. I no longer had the time or energy to be the one to make plans for winter break parties or group trips to the movies.

Before I left I also peeked at the counselor list. Butthole wasn't on it again, but this year I had a feeling he wasn't going to be showing up at all.

It was also unfortunate to find out that Gene finally followed through on his plan to retire, but was just waiting for camp to get going so he could step down. Julie was hoping that Gene's departure would land her as The Park's new head supervisor. She was the best candidate for the job with her fifteen years of experience. They rejected her application three times.

For a moment I thought my summer would remain intact, but one week before camp started, Julie was offered a supervisor position at a different park. Even with camp fast approaching she had to take the better job, and to my dismay, leave camp in the hands of someone new. The Park wouldn't be the same without her.

The first week of camp was strange. Julie was gone and Gene was only involved part time. Kevin, who was a full time employee at The Park for years, took over as camp director. He was even younger than Julie and not much older than some of us. But never for a second did we try to test his authority, not with the amount of respect we still owed to Gene and Julie.

"Hi, I'm here to sign in my son Michael," a forty-year-old looking father with a black mustache was wondering what to do next.

"No problem," I said. "Just find his name on the clip-board."

"Well, he's only ten," he said to me in a rush, "so I went to the nine and ten year old group first, but they sent me over here." I looked spitefully over at James.

"Okay, let me see if I have his emergency form." I whipped out the binder so it could see one of its few useful moments this summer. Everything was a blur as I flipped through the names. "Yeah I found him, he's in my group."

"Well, I don't see why," the dad said to me eyeing his son. "He is only ten and I think it might be better for him to be with the ten year old group."

"Oh," I looked back down to the sheet. "He is only ten. I'm sorry about the mix up."

"That's no problem, I think it's just easier for everyone this way."

"I agree," I told him. "You can actually take this form back over to James and he will add Michael to his list." I handed him the emergency form clearly marked 'ten year old.'

"Thanks again," he said guiding his son back in the other direction.

"Yeah, sorry about the mix up." Michael and his dad walked over to James's group. Other than having one less camper to worry about, I wouldn't think twice about Michael for weeks.

Kevin turned out to be not only a fun boss, but also someone who held his ground a little more when it came to dealing with the campers. Julie and Gene both had worked at The Park for so long, they knew the parents of most of the kids. This helped those campers goof off and break rules without really being punished. Kevin ran camp by the book. If a girl was caught swearing, she got a letter home. When two of my boys got into a fight, they got suspended from camp. When the younger kids would poop in the pool, Kevin made the lifeguards empty it out and clean it.

"Pick up that shit!" he would say.

"Yes sir," the lifeguards would answer.

"Empty the pool," he would say.

"Yes sir," they would answer.

"Scrub away the shit," he would say.

"Please no more!" they would answer.

Kevin had a somewhat shaky persona during training, but by the end of week one he really had a feel for his job. I had a similar progression with my group. I still had the oldest boy group, but I now had some student teaching experience. On day one the kids were finishing a game of kickball when I tried to lay down the foundations for an obedient group.

"Pick up that shit!" I yelled.

"Fuck you," the campers replied. *So bad.*

On day three I was using positive reinforcement to my advantage. "Pick up that shit and I will let you choose the next game we play."

"I hate you," the campers said. *Progress.*

Finally, by day five my teaching skills started to pay off. "Can you please pick up that stuff or I will tell Kevin you guys don't want to listen."

"Please don't tell Kevin, he hates us," they said. *A break-through!*

"Then get moving," I demanded, now in control.

"Yes sir!" they said.

Gene officially retired after the first week of camp. At the time, no one was hired to replace him as supervisor. I thought it was fitting, because physically and metaphorically, replacing Gene was nearly impossible. I had lost two important role models in a couple of weeks, and while some people would be glad that they had no one looking over their shoulder at work, I missed Gene and Julie everyday.

I was on my own during my fifth year at camp. I would spend time with James's group and receive Cesar's help when he wasn't working with play camp, but I generally ran the group myself. From the first day I knew I was going to be in for a long year.

Mikey and Peter were two eleven year old campers that were in James's group last year. From what I knew they were two of his best kids. As it turned out, they were the only two good kids in my group of twenty-five. When I asked them to line up, they did. Time to eat, they ate. Play football, they organized the game for me. They were more useful than my counselors, Gabe and John Paul, and I was developing a profound liking for them.

Group control was so difficult at times that I could only convince four kids to play football. America was reaching the peak of the video game revolution and most campers wanted to sit around the first few weeks playing their Game Boys, so naturally, we sent a letter home banning them. Then my boys took out the little bit of energy they had on each other, by means of fighting. The first weeks were extensive and frustrating to say the least, but I still had Mikey and Peter to lean on for support. They helped me persuade, half the time to no avail, the other campers to participate. Without the group, even the good athletes were going to be stuck the entire summer sitting around. Even when the usually reliable capture the flag turned into a game of six versus six, Mikey and Peter kept their composure. I was getting paid regardless of camper participation. Mikey and Peter were not as lucky. If their peers wouldn't play, they couldn't either. And, there was only so much I could do to entertain them.

At times I would take a group of boys to play knockout on the basketball court while the rest of my group moped around in the shade. It seemed most of the days that we played knockout my now yellow camp shirt would be soaked in sweat from all the excitement, but our game would have to be stopped because a fight broke out between two campers. Mikey and Peter couldn't catch a break.

At least after camp I could try and make up for lost time with them. Peter would usually stay five or ten extra minutes each day to hang out and play catch. We would talk about our families and school. It was nice to know that some eleven year olds were intelligent enough to hold a conversation.

Mikey waited for his sister, who was a counselor, to get off work everyday before he would head home. When Peter would leave, Mikey and I seized the opportunity to converse by ourselves, or with the few remaining campers, and talk about more lax subjects, new video games and ideas for upcoming camp days. The conversations were fun and I was glad to be able to spend time getting to know some of my campers on individual levels.

July '05

I turned twenty-one during year five at The Park. Now I really felt old. Drinking with sixteen year olds is not that bad when you yourself are under age. Now it was bad…and creepy…and illegal.

The weeks following my twenty first birthday were great at camp. Julia was now in full swing with her group and she looked to me for advice. I would help her with game ideas during work and talk with her about high school drama at night.

I really took a liking to helping her. Sometimes my advice was nothing more than guesswork. Other times I was speaking from experience. What mattered to me was that I was there for her when she needed me. I could be a teacher for Julia and the other younger rec. leaders. Show them how to run a group properly without getting stressed. She repaid me with stories she would tell everyone else about us growing up.

"I remember being in front of Hailey's house when I was about eight years old, and Vince came over and started yelling at me because of something I was doing. He was what, thirteen at the time, and Hailey and I thought he was joking…so we kept laughing and playing and stuff. But then Vince started throwing pine cones at me, and Frodo, Nick, and Stephen just watched it happen."

Caitlin looked at me with her mouth opened, half in amazement and half trying not to laugh. "Do you remember this?"

Usually the stories my cousin told my friends seemed made up. This one was unfortunately true. "Yeah, I remember it. I don't think I threw the pine cones for 'no reason,' like she says."

"Yeah whatever Bobby, this is my story," Julia reminded us and continued. "So I was trying to run away from him and his pine cones, but he was so much older. I told him to stop throwing the pine cones because they hurt, but I think that made him more mad and he ran up to me and started to choke me." Caitlin was trying to hold in a laugh knowing that Julia came out of the situation alive, but deep down I knew she wanted to run for her life. "He was laughing the whole time with his friends who were still sitting there watching. I went home and cried all night."

I was shaking my head in question of the story's facts. "Can I defend myself?" I asked the two of them. No one said otherwise, so I began. "First off, you were the worst little cousin ever. Because you were an only child you thought it was okay to try and boss me around. Whenever you came over you would steal the remote control from me and beat me up."

"Oh my god Bobby!" Julia said, appalled at herself. "Was I really like that?" Now she was laughing herself.

"Well because I was older it was hard to defend myself without making you cry. Plus, your mom always told me to beat you up if you were messing with me."

"Yeah, but what about that day Julia just told me about?" Caitlin seemed to know I was avoiding the memory in question.

"Well, I remember that day," I began. "What I remember is Julia being mean to me, again, and I warned her a million times to stop or I would hurt her. But, as is her nature, she didn't know when to stop…so I started throwing the pinecones. I was probably trying to impress my friends. Then you were yelling at me and calling me names so I stopped throwing the cones and choked you."

"See, I told you," Julia said, proud of the truth coming out.

"I was stupid and young, but I know I never would have done that if I knew you were so scared. We always wrestled at my house and I guess I didn't know this time was different."

"Yeah Bobby! I was having nightmares for years."

"I'm sorry Jules."

"Haha, come on Vinny Dude," Julia said cheerfully. "I probably woke up the next morning fine."

"Yeah but you remember it still now," I reminded her.

"Don't worry, it never made me love you any less."

"Aw, I wish I had this sappy shit with my family," Caitlin commented. "All of my memories growing up are about being choked."

"Really Bobby!?" Julia asked in a now serious tone.

Caitlin looked at her with a lost sense of respect, "No you fool. Yeah my family sucks, but I never got choked. No one in my family is as mean as Vince."

"That's it, I'm going to find my campers," I said, rising from the stairs. "I hope both of you have a wonderful day." I headed outside to wait for my arriving campers.

Later that day Stephen came by The Park with two baseball mitts and a ball. I would go weeks without seeing him, but we always picked up our friendship right where it left off.

"Can you play?" he asked me, knowing very well that I might not be able to. I think it was hard for him to sit at home while most of his friends, including his brother, were working at camp together.

"Sure, give me five minutes." I organized a game of soccer for the boys and Cesar agreed to ref the game so I could play some catch with Stephen. This was one of the main perks of the job, having bosses that were so down to earth that I was able to have visitors from outside of camp every now and then.

"So how is everything?" I asked him. Stephen's life just felt so foreign and interesting to me that I wanted to hear all about it.

"Pretty good man," he said mid throw. "Been playing a lot of baseball recently."

"Seems like it." I had noticed his improvement just from our simple game of catch. "Have you talked to Frodo at all?"

He tossed a pop fly to me, which made me take a few steps back and shade my eyes with my glove. "Not really," he said as I came down with the ball. "He spends most of his time with his Ignatius friends." I threw the ball back to him, almost sending it over his head and onto Irving Park Road. "We did play some Whiffle ball the other day in front of his house though. Me, him, Dale, Nick, and some other people."

"Yeah, Nick told me," I said, snagging a curveball from the air. "We should play again sometime soon."

"Hey man, I'm down." he said. "I sit around all day and watch baseball."

"Must be great."

"It's not bad."

Our conversation went back and forth like this for about twenty minutes. I asked about his friends and girls, he asked me to trade him Alex Rodriguez in fantasy baseball. I also realized that Stephen, my first student ever, had grown up right before my eyes.

He left as the soccer game ended, but the excitement of the day was not over. Joey, the class clown of my group, approached me with a problem. "One of James's kids, a ten year old, is screaming at us," he said.

"Why?"

"I don't know."

"So it's just for fun?" I was beginning to interrogate him. The necessity of putting preteen boys in their place was high on my priority list. *Someone has to teach them.*

"I think so Vince. He looks like the kind of kid who would scream for fun."

"So when I ask him what his problem is, he will say nothing?"

"Okay, okay, it's because they took his hat."

"Who did?" I asked, now heading towards the scene with Joey.

"Not me, but they gave it back to him already." Just then I heard what sounded like a baby lion trying to roar. At least how they sound in *Lion King.*

"Arrrr! You guys are stupid!" the manic child yelled. "Arrr! How would you like it if I took your favorite hat?"

"Relax, we can talk about this somewhere quiet if you want," Joey said before I could even open my mouth. *You cannot let yourself laugh at this.*

"Calm down," Marco said, my camper who was probably the culprit. "Just breathe kid." It seemed a few of my campers were attempting to act as the child's shrink. The problem was, they weren't offering genuine help, they were poking fun at the situation.

"No, you calm down! My dad gave me this hat and he said I can't let it get dirty and now it's dirty and he is going to be mad at me!"

"Who is that kid?" I asked James who was now observing the situation.

"That's Michael. Remember? The kid who was supposed to be in *your* group, but you sent him to me the first day?"

Wow, how one insignificant event can change an entire summer. "Yeah, I remember now. Is he always like this?"

"Sir? Always."

"Wait, he's *the* crazy one? The camper you are always complaining about to Kevin?"

"Yes sir, the craziest."

"Well he is ten, and you do have the ten year old boys…so technically I didn't give him to you," now I was poking fun at James. "*I'm* glad things turned out for the best in the end."

Just then Michael started chasing Marco and screaming uncontrollably. "I hate you sir," he responded with.

It was the third week of camp and I finally felt I was successfully using some of my new teaching skills to my advantage. I had come up with art games for my campers to do, which the whole group attempted and actually enjoyed. For four years I was clueless when it came to art time. Sometimes I would try to follow the projects the rest of camp was doing, but my boys were too old to care about glitter pens and Popsicle stick houses. More often than not, that part of our schedule was ignored.

Now I had groups playing Pictionary for prizes. The participation was always one hundred percent for these games because, while it was art, it was still a competition that didn't require exercise. An intense thirty-minute session Tuesday, capped by the group's drawings of 'Chicago' and 'air,' had settled into a near three-way tie. Cesar laughed that my 'air' suggestion was answered after one camper drew two wavy lines, but his 'Chicago' took the kids nearly the entire minute to figure out. Either way, the tiebreaker needed to be well thought out.

"This is the last round and it is worth two points." I considered multiple ideas before calling over the final campers to draw. I whispered to them, "I want you to draw Dale's mom."

"Who the hell is Dale?" asked Joey.

"Um, me and him were only your rec. leaders last year," I informed him, never sure if Joey was serious.

"Oh, Dale the rec. leader," Joey said. "How can I draw his mom?"

Maybe it was too hard.

"It's easy," Peter responded, shaking his head at the stupidity of his fellow campers.

All they had to do was get the group to guess Dale first, before moving on to the mother part. "It's the last one, it's supposed to be hard." I felt I needed to defend my choice. "Ready, set, go!"

Cesar walked over to me as the pencils hit the paper. "What are they drawing?"

"Dale's mom," I answered.

"You are an idiot," he told me.

"I take that as a compliment."

The two of us looked around at each of the three groups' drawings. It was our job to listen for the answers being shouted out by the team members who were guessing. The artists were sketching as quickly and accurately as possible. Joey was drawing a picture of an old woman with a purse. Peter was drawing Dale the best he could. He was thinking outside the box. The third artist was drawing a woman yelling at a boy. Shouts of "grandma," "prostitute," and "John Elway" filled the room. Finally Peter's team figured out his drawing and claimed first place. I passed out victory Popsicles to each member of his group and asked Cesar to take them outside.

I was cleaning up the art room and admiring the cleverness of some of my boys' drawings when Kevin came downstairs. He wanted to know if I would be able to attend the end of the year banquet Gene was having for us. I was surprised to be having this conversation so early in the camp year. Still, I knew that nothing was more important than giving Gene a sendoff, so I agreed that I would attend.

"When is it going to be?" I asked as he scribbled down my confirmation.

"Well Gene said the last Friday of camp. He wants to know who is interested because if no one wants to do it, then he won't bother."

"I will definitely be there."

"Okay, I'll let him know," Kevin insured me. "Do you know where Cesar is?"

"Yeah, he just took the group outside."

Kevin exited the art room and headed into the main field in search of Cesar and the rest of my group. I tossed away the few remaining scraps from our game and followed Kevin towards the north softball field. He was already in discussion with Cesar about the banquet. My campers were standing against the backstop, which traditionally meant a game of kickball was about to get underway.

"Did Cesar break you into teams yet?" I asked Joey who was putting out the bases.

"Not yet, he just asked me to set these up," he answered.

Most of our time was usually wasted on gathering players and picking teams for games that were short and unfulfilling. To my surprise, the group seemed ready to play. "Joey, you stay in the field."

"Okay," he said.

I walked over to the group and Cesar joined me as his conversation with Kevin ended. "Did you pick teams?" he asked.

"Ha, no, I was just wondering if you did," I replied. "We're better off getting the game going now, before half the campers change their minds and sit down."

"Yeah definitely," Cesar concurred.

"Listen up!" Now I had their attention. "Let me have Peter on the team batting first, Mikey you can join Joey in the field. Marco you stay on this team, Andre you're out there." The next few minutes were spent splitting up the group to make even teams, figuring out positions and batting order, and controlling the boys' urges to kick the dry infield dirt into the air. Finally, Joey rolled out the first pitch and we were on our way to forty minutes of good old fashion camp kickball.

With occasional successful games wedged in between hours of down time, one thing was unquestioned, my campers were hooked on Pictionary. We played a few times a week for the rest of camp. When I asked the kids to draw Harry Potter, a whole new realm of opportunity opened. I was blindsided by my boys' love for the *Harry Potter* series. Six months earlier I began to read the books because it seemed everyone I knew was reading them. Now my campers and I were having hour-long conversations about *The Half Blood Prince*. I even contemplated a *Harry Potter* based talent show but settled on an ode to 1980s music. It put a smile on my face knowing that I was able to form another bond with my campers. So often sports and video games were the only ways for me and my campers to find common interests. Yet, I had somehow managed to link us through art and reading. Maybe I was going to be a better teacher than I thought.

Over my sixteen summers at camp I learned that repetition could be both beneficial and destructive. Kids needed some structure to control their questions and impulses, yet some well-timed spontaneity could work wonders. I knew personally that I had been playing the same games for as long as I could remember. First I learned them, then I played them, then I taught them. I told myself that the games themselves must be fun because I kept playing them, but perhaps I was just trapped in a routine. Kickball is a great sport, but playing it more than once a week is over doing it. The same goes for dodgeball, hockey, and softball. Enough already.

Enter funball and Joe Voigt's creation, Voigtball. Each game is simple. Funball is basically the baseball game piggy, where one person hits fly balls to a hoard of waiting outfielders. However, the ball being batted is a large rubber ball. Three catches of the ball in the air or on one bounce earns a chance to bat yourself. However, the proper field is essential. We played next to the playground in an area filled with several tall trees. Not enough to get in the way of the game, but enough to help ricochet the flying rubber ball in varying directions. Twenty colliding campers, counselors, and rec. leaders, namely Dale, James, and Joe Voigt, made the game just as violent as tackle football. Brad Pitt had his fight club, the eleven and twelve year old boys had their funball. I resorted to funball a few times a week, sending the lazy boys to the playground where we could still keep on eye on them. I will never look at the grass patch that became our funball field the same way again.

Voigtball, on the other hand, is more casual game. Just find a place outside with lots of seating, and bounce a basketball off of the ground and into a garbage can. Teams of players alternate throws, or 'at bats,' until each player has gone one time. This concludes one inning. Each made shot is one point. Games are nine innings long. Simple enough.

And as addicting as crack.

Voigtball games took over camp. Softball, kickball, and hockey were replaced. Rec. leaders ignored their campers. Campers set up their own Voigtball "courts." Even Nick found time to get away from his own duties and play a game every now and then. I recall watching an intense game at the end of a day that pitted Cesar, Nick, and Joe Voigt against James, Derek, and Dale. Parents were already waiting for their boys as half the camp crowded around the playground benches to watch their rec. leaders drain shot after shot. For the first time in years campers did not want to go home.

It was reminiscent of a better time at camp. When campers liked sports and rec. leaders joked around all day. Camp did not have the same feel as a few years back when it seemed I was friends with everyone on the staff. Now there were rec. leaders who didn't even talk to each other, who barely knew each other's names. Still, these Voigtball games were a fine reminder of years gone by.

Nick was working late shifts during the week and struggled to find time to hang out the way he used to. Even with his schedule, I still could count on him showing up for the MLB homerun derby. The guy rec. leaders would come over to my house, order pizza, and watch the always too long homerun contest. Out of the eight derby contestants each of us would choose one to support for the evening. Just as he did with the Cubs, Derek rooted with his heart instead of his head. He is the only one to ever pick a player who went homerless.

Originally, watching the derby at my house was one of the few sober traditions we had as rec. leaders. Now I was noticing that most of the activities we did during the summer didn't involve drinking. WhirlyBall replaced partying at my house. We went to the beach with a cooler filled with Pepsi and Dr. Pepper and not Bud Light. Maybe it was because most of the rec. leading staff was becoming teachers that we felt the need to keep the drinking to a minimum. Or maybe without Big White and Katie around, no one found drinking as interesting. Either way, hanging out with the guys during the derby was more fun anyway.

Dale and Nick arrived and were caught up discussing a head shaving idea they had. Both wanted to shave it all off but neither had the will to do it first. James was fed up with their bickering so he took matters into his own hands.

"I'm going to get my clippers, and when I get back we are all shaving our heads," he bolted out my basement door to his car.

"This is going to get interesting," Nick pointed out, piercing Dale with his stare. "Look what you've done."

"Me?" Dale asked. "You're the one who thought of the whole idea."

"Yeah, but now James is involved," Nick complained, knowing that everyone of us understood his pain.

James returned and three minutes of deliberating was put to a halt when Stephen walked in and forced the issue. "If you bitches aren't going to do it, then I will," he said.

"Wait wait, I want to go first," Dale said, sitting in the designated barber chair.

"I want to let you know now," I said, making sure my words were heard, "that before any of this begins, all of you better help me clean up the hair before the derby is over."

"Sheebs, that's going to be a lot of hair," Dale stated obviously. He now had a towel wrapped around his bare neck. "Okay I'm ready."

James plugged in the clippers and flicked to the appropriate length. "This is the length I always use," he said, rubbing his own head to show us. "Is that okay?"

Dale looked up at James's hair and made a grimacing face. "How about you don't go that short on me."

"Fine, Dale," James mocked. "For you I will go one longer." Dale was facing the T.V. as the first round of the contest was underway. James motioned the clippers to a length of five, satisfying Dale's wishes. Then he looked over at me, smiled, and rolled the length back down to four. Anything for a laugh.

Three hours and six shaved heads later, Bobby Abreu was finally crowned the derby winner. We chatted for a while before everyone left, mostly about how another year went by and once again no one correctly picked the winner. Cesar and

Derek were already starting the inevitable conversation, about this being their last summer at The Park. Nick, because of his other responsibilities, was barely around to begin with, and with James and I concentrating on school and teaching, it seemed that only Dale and Joe Voigt would be working next summer. I guess the torch was being passed at the time and I didn't even know it.

Once I had a camper get sent to the hospital after being hit by an ice cream cart. His leg was torn open so deep that white muscle was exposed. I had almost been fired for invoking corporal punishment on campers. And even another time, I nearly lost my mind when I caught my boys throwing rocks at the animals at the zoo. But, up until the end of my fifth year as a rec. leader, I had never lost a camper.

My boys always had permission to step out the back gym door and get a drink from the water fountain. It was unfair to make them seek me out every time they were thirsty.

As we headed to lunch I took a head count of my group. Twenty-two here today, but I only counted twenty-one. I checked my calculations two more times to be sure. Still one short. *Someone must be in the bathroom or still getting water.* I had J. P. fetch my clipboard just to be sure. In the meantime I figured asking the group couldn't hurt. "Boys, can someone check the water fountain to see if anyone is out there?"

Mikey ran to the back door and peeked out. "No one Vince," he said.

"Okay, thanks," I said, hoping that our missing kid was just a counting error on my part. "Get your lunches and go down to the art room to eat."

J. P. was coming up as I was headed downstairs and he handed me the clipboard.

"We're headed back down that way anyway," I informed him. "Grab your lunch and come down after the campers have theirs."

"Can I have two lunches?" he asked.

"Sure, J. P."

I waited till I sat down to eat to look at my sign in sheet. Twice I counted the names, each time twenty-two. The campers filed in and I checked off their names on my list. Joey, here. Sasquel, here. Marco, here. Then it hit me. Jesse, the camper I should have thought of first, had asked to get water half way through our pinball game and I didn't recall seeing him after that.

"HEY, HAS ANYONE SEEN JESSE?" I was now standing and the group was at attention.

"I saw him during gym time," Marco said.

"Did anyone see him leave the gym?" I asked.

"Yeah," Joey answered. "He was mad about his Game Boy and then he got up and left."

"You saw him leave and didn't come tell me?"

"I didn't know he was like, leaving forever. I thought he was just going outside to get water or something."

"John Paul, go look over by the Women's Building for him. Gabe," I said, turning towards my other counselor, "see if you can find him anywhere else."

Cesar was just leaving play camp, so I found him coming across the field. "Hey, I need you to watch the guys right now. I have to call Jesse's house, he's gone."

"Figures you would be the first to lose one," he said.

"Thanks." I went upstairs to find Kevin, but only Ashley was in the office. "Where's Kevin?"

"He's not coming in today," she said, much to my dismay.

"Okay, well here's my problem. One of my campers, Jesse, left the group about twenty minutes ago. I have some counselors looking for him, but I want to call his house now so his parents are aware of the situation."

"I'll look for his number." At this point I was still certain that Jesse would show up in a few minutes or had just walked home because he was so upset over his Game Boy. I was lucky enough to have the oldest boys, and Jesse in particular, lived only a few blocks away and walked home everyday. She found the number for me and I picked up the phone to call.

"Hi, this is Vince, I am Jesse's rec. leader at Independence Park."

"Oh hi Vince, I'm Jesse's mom," the female voice on the other line spoke. "What did he do now?"

"Actually, I was hoping he came home recently."

"No, why?"

"Well, he got into a small fight during gym time over his Game Boy. I was unaware of this, but I let him go outside to get a drink of water and he never returned."

"How long ago was this?"

"About twenty or thirty minutes ago. I have counselors looking for him but they are not allowed to leave the park."

"Thanks for the call. I'll have my daughter wait here in case he comes home and I'll drive around looking for him. He might be at one of his friends' houses in the neighborhood. Call my cell phone if he shows up. Do you have the number?" I checked to see if the number was on the emergency form.

"Yeah it's here. I'll keep you posted."

J.P. and Gabe came back without any sign of Jesse. The whole situation was turning into a mess. With Kevin gone and no Gene and Julie, there was really no one in charge. The camp director of our therapeutic camp was also gone, on a field trip, so Ashley was manning the office by herself. Ashley and I made calls to Kevin, but he was stranded an hour away. It was Murphy's Law at its finest.

I was starting to hope he wandered home when his mom showed up at the park house.

"Did he come back yet?" she asked me. *Not Good.*

"No, not yet," I answered. "Most of the time the kids will just go back home, but I guess not today."

"I don't know what to do," her tone suddenly changed from mad to concerned. "I checked all of his friends' houses that I know of. I even checked McDonald's."

I thought quickly. "I'm going to call the police and let them know of our situation."

When the police arrived they talked to me for a few minutes. All they could really do was wait for camp to end and hope Jesse would just go home and act like he never left camp.

The next two hours lingered for what seemed like days, and besides a few failed attempts to reach Kevin, not much changed.

Finally, with camp just minutes away from ending, Kevin showed up. He was shocked to find the situation still unresolved.

"How come I wasn't called again?"

"We tried Kevin, it went straight to voice mail," I said. "We left you messages." He pulled out his phone to check. "I have no messages. Are you sure you called?"

"Yes, me and Ashley called."

"Well our district supervisor, will be here soon. She is not going to be happy." Kevin was trying to figure out what to do next. "I think you handled the situation as best as possible," he said to me, "but she won't think so." *Today is the greatest day ever.* "No matter what you say, she will find a way to fault you. If you say that you had a counselor watching him, she will say that you should have had two counselors watching. If you tell her that he went to get water and ran away, she will say that you should never let kids get water alone. If you say that he wasn't alone, she will say that you need to bring the whole group to the water fountain."

"Really?" I said nervously. "But all those forms at training and everything I have ever learned is that you must send your campers in pairs, nothing ever about taking whole group trips to the bathroom and water fountain."

"Trust me I know," he said. We practiced what to say for the next five minutes, eyeing the clock, waiting for her arrival.

The second she arrived, the yelling started. "Who was in charge here?" she bellowed.

"I was gone on an emergency and called it in," Kevin began to explain the entirety of the chaotic event. "I tried to get out of it but I had to attend to a personal matter."

"So that's it?" the district supervisor said angrily. "You can't come in so the place is left unattended? Where was the therapeutic camp?"

"They were on a trip this morning…left before I called in," Kevin said, staying much more calm than I would have.

"If you knew no one would be here you HAVE to come in!"

"But I didn't know that. Their trip was a last second thing. When I called to let everyone know I would be late, I was not informed about the park being unsupervised. No one told me about the therapeutic camp being gone."

"Who answered the phone?" she asked.

"Rich, the engineer."

"So are you blaming him?"

"Not at all, I am saying it was a huge misunderstanding, with lack of communication on all parts."

"This is UNACCEPTABLE!" I thought her head was going to explode.

"It has been very difficult running both play camp and day camp by myself here, everyday, without a supervisor. Since Gene and Julie left, we have been waiting for a replacement to help out." Now I couldn't see who she could possibly be mad at. It was a *management* mistake that our park was left without supervisors. Her mistake.

"The situation with that does not make what is happening here acceptable." Now she turned to me. "The boy is in your group?"

"Yes, he's twelve."

"Have you ever heard of counting your kids?"

"I'm sorry. I did count them and that is when I realized he was missing."

"And now three hours later he still is!"

"I called his parents, the police, and tried to get in touch with Kevin as soon as I found out."

"Once three fifteen hits I am going to have to call the news stations and issue an Amber Alert for a possible kidnapping."

I looked at the clock. It was five after three.

Originally I was mad that Jesse left. Then, I was mad that I was getting blamed for it. As the clock continued to tick, I stopped being mad and started to worry. *What if something did happen to him?* I didn't think I could ever forgive myself.

With each passing minute the tension in the room heightened. After my district supervisor made three or four calls to various authorities, the office phone started to ring.

Kevin reached for it, "Independence Park, Kevin speaking." He listened for a few seconds before responding. "He's home?" Kevin asked. "Okay, I will let everyone over here know. I'm so very sorry. Okay…that's okay…alright, goodbye."

"He's home?" our supervisor asked.

"Yeah. He went to a friend's house and decided to sneak home when camp got out."

"We got lucky here people," she said. "I will be back tomorrow to check up on the situation."

And that was it. The district supervisor was gone. Jesse was back at home. And I would never talk to either one of them again.

August '05

Caitlin preferred spending time with her sisters instead of a group of friends. After camp and on weekends, as much as she appeared content to just hang out with my friends, there was probably too much ESPN and *Smash Brothers* for her liking. Megan and Joanne were around, but they still weren't friends she had personal relationships with.

Then there was Cristina, who Caitlin had worked with at camp for years. However, Cristina was not someone who was around during the school year. It created this friends versus family dynamic in our relationship, but there was still one last hope, Julia.

"So, how come you never hang out with me and Caitlin?" I asked her during the last week of camp.

"Oh my God Bobby! I would hang out, it's just that Brian is too lazy to come out with me," Julia explained. I knew her boyfriend was shy when it came to our family.

"No really, you should come by this weekend," I told her. "Caitlin is always around, and Megan too, but then it's like six guys and the girls get outnumbered."

"Not Friday right, because we have Gene's party thing," she reminded me.

"Yeah I know, Saturday."

"Hell yeah I'll come by," she said. "Are we swimming in your pool?"

"Of course." If I would have known a simple conversation was all it took to get Julia to be part of the group, I would have invited her over well before the last week of camp. It didn't take long for her and Caitlin to click, which made the socializing easier for me. I did not have to worry about Caitlin being bored because now she had someone else to talk to. This situation also improved Caitlin's mood towards hanging out with my family. Julia is on both sides of my family, since her mom and my mom are sisters and her dad and my dad are brothers, and she was always there to talk Caitlin into hanging out.

As the last days of camp wound down and our talent show went off with success once again, I began to grow nostalgic. With an impending summer filled with class in Champaign next year, this was going to be my last year. Peter and Mikey promised they would return for their last year as campers, which too often kids tended not to do. I said my goodbye to day camp the same way I started it, with James by my side.

"I don't think I will be back next year either," he said to me.

"Hey, it had to end sometime," I said inevitably.

"I just don't want it to."

"This really is the worst day of my life."

"I know how you feel."

I knew The Park would always be there for me to visit, so even though I was devastated by the idea of 'retiring,' I kept a small amount of hope.

Gene's end of the year party was at La Villa, the same place we ordered pizza from every week in the summer. Caitlin and I arrived on time at seven. I pulled my same red Mercury Mystique into the parking spot nearest the front doors and turned off the car. I stashed the detachable face for my radio into my glove compartment and pulled out a white piece of paper from it. I opened it up and read the information in the top section.

Cooperating teacher: Mrs. Owens.

Clinical Location: Monticello, Illinois.

I folded the paper back up. "I hope she is cool," I said to Caitlin forcing the form into my pocket. "I need to put this with the rest of my stuff before I lose it."

"Is that your teaching thing?" she asked as she opened her door. "What's her name again?"

"Mrs. Owens." I closed my door and walked towards the restaurant. "I can't believe in one month I will be student teaching in her classroom."

"You'll love it," she said leaning up at me for a kiss.

We kissed softly and I opened the door for her. "I'm sure I will," I said.

We were the first ones there and felt somewhat awkward seeing only Gene sitting at the bar. Gene never intimidated me, but we always had something to talk about. Now it seemed we had to find a common interest other than The Park.

I sat next to Gene so that Caitlin wouldn't have to be even more uncomfortable. I decided right then and there that I had spent too many years of my life knowing Gene to be timid around him.

"So how is retired life?" I asked him to break the ice.

"Not as great as I thought," he began. "It's nice to see my grandkids everyday, but I find myself golfing a little too much." He took a drink from his beer and set it back on the bar. "Do you want something?" he asked us. "It's all on me tonight."

I looked at Caitlin to get her drink order while I decided my own in my head. Alcohol had lost its appeal when I turned twenty-one. It happens to a large portion of people. Once the excitement of illegally drinking is over, you realize you would rather be spending your time productively.

I debated, *Pepsi or beer, beer or Pepsi,* over and over and stalled by asking Caitlin again what she wanted. She told me a Sprite, and even though I wanted a Pepsi, I felt by drinking a beer I would be showing respect to Gene. I know I wouldn't want to throw a party and have my friends come over and drink Pepsi, so I ordered one Sprite and one Bud Light.

The bartender filled Caitlin's cup and popped the lid off of my beer. He placed the drinks in front of us and I immediately took a sip.

"Are you not twenty-one yet Caitlin?" Gene asked when he saw her drink.

She put down her glass. "Not for three more years," she told him proudly. I think she liked telling everyone how young she was when I was around. It gave her a sense of accomplishment, like she was so hot that she bagged herself a guy three years older. That, or she liked making fun of me and how I had to date someone three years younger.

"It seems like you have been around forever though," Gene said to her. "Fuck, eighteen, makes me feel old." He stopped to do some mental calculations. "I was working at

The Park when you were two years old. That's not even count-ing where I worked before Independence."

Gene looked towards the front door. Kevin walked in with a few other year round employees. We all said hello and they took seats at the bar around us.

"Is this it?" Gene asked Kevin. "Anyone else coming tonight?" A nervous feeling began to form in the pit of my stomach. Gene was a great boss and he was throwing us an all you can eat and drink thank you party for all the years we shared together, and five people showed up?

I pulled out my phone to check the time. It was seven thirty, if anyone else was coming they were already half an hour late. "Where is everyone?" I whispered to Caitlin, scared Gene might hear and feel even worse.

She shrugged her shoulders back at me and said, "I thought James and Nick were coming."

"I'm going to call them now," I told her putting the phone to my ear. As I waited for James to answer, Gene was moving our group from the bar to the small banquet area he reserved. James picked up. "Hey, where are you at? There are only a few of us here."

"Settle down sir, I'm parking the car. Where do I go in?" he asked.

"We are right in the front doors, on the right side of the bar," I answered. "Do you know where Nick and Derek are?"

"I just talked to Derek, he was picking up Jaimie, and Nick should be here soon." I was relieved. At least some peo-ple cared to show up.

"Okay, see you in a little bit." I hung up the phone and followed Caitlin to our chairs. There were seats for twenty-five or thirty people arranged around four long white tables.

"Where is your buddy Nick?" Gene asked me from the next table over.

I took my seat and put my phone in my pocket. "He'll be here soon. Everyone else is on their way too."

"Well, we can order now and they can order when they get here," he said. "We shouldn't have to wait any longer, it's already past seven thirty."

I searched the table for a menu and ended up just looking on with Caitlin. James walked in, shook Gene's hand, and sat down next to me. "Where did you get that menu?" he asked looking around.

"This is Caitlin's," I said motioning to the menu in front of me. He got up and gave me a look like he was offended by what I said. He strolled to another table, picked up a stack of menus and returned to his seat next to me, slamming the menus on the table.

"I don't know if I have ever eaten anything besides the pizza from here," said James. "It all sounds so good. 'Creamy alfredo sauce poured over chicken breast and fettuccini pasta. Served with garlic bread.' I think I just had an orgasm."

"Wow sir," Caitlin commented. "Inappropriate."

The waiter came around asking us for our orders and I decided on the chicken alfredo. James's description must have been better than I thought. As the waiter made his way down the row, Nick, Dale, Derek, and Jaimie walked in. They sat down and we promptly passed down menus so they could order before the waiter finished.

Nick chose the seat on James's left, between us and the other year round employees, including Gene. He was the best person to bridge the gap because he was the only one who had worked both day camp and year round.

I talked with Derek about his plans for senior year. I knew he was unsure if he could graduate in May and wondered if this would be his last year at The Park. He told me everything was still up in the air but that most likely he would be in Arizona for summer school.

Cesar and Grace joined us before the food came and they were bombarded with the same question as everyone else,

"Are you working next summer?" Cesar refused to answer until he ordered, so we gave him two minutes of peace. Grace said that she was returning. Cesar looked at her and I watched them whisper back and forth. Things between them were difficult this year. Their relationship had fizzled a few years back and now they were trying to become friends again.

Cesar passed off his menu to the waiter and looked back at our wondering faces. James, Caitlin, and I were still watching him, waiting for his answer. When he noticed our stares, he smiled from the awkwardness and said, "I plan on graduating in December and getting a job as a trainer. I hope I'm not back next year, because if I am, then I didn't get a job I wanted."

"Well let's hope you don't get a job," Caitlin retorted. I never heard one negative comment be so positive. Out of all of the rec. leaders, he was the only one that everyone liked. Cesar had been working at camp since my first year. We shared a group many times and had developed a good friendship year round because of that. It would suck to say goodbye to all of that.

Julia and Cristina came a few minutes after the waiter left, and Ashley shortly after them. As they settled in and ordered, I looked around the room at all the familiar faces. It may not have been the same staff I started my first year with, but I really had no right to complain. These people were my best friends and I was going to cherish what would probably be my last evening with them. The conversations and laughter made it hard to think, or maybe that was the beer. The food arrived and I had no intentions of pacing myself, so I dove right in. Everyone else did likewise. Twenty minutes later, half eaten dinners remained in front of us as we reclined in our seats to ease the pressure off of our stomachs.

Kevin convinced us to start trying the foreign beers on the menu. From barely talking to drinking down a whole menu, our new boss and his staff had come along way since last summer. We drank *Heineken* for the Netherlands and *Corona* for Mexico. *Guinness* for Ireland, *Peroni* for Italy, and *Sam Adams* for America. After touring half the world, I learned an important lesson for my future: Italy should stick to their wine.

We were making small talk when Gene stood up and raised his beer. "I see that everyone is done eating so I wanted to make a toast." *Oh boy. This man has meant so much to me for so long that whatever words he says will affect me more than anyone else.* If I were alone right then, I would have started crying. He continued, "For sixteen years I ran Independence Park and I have had many staffs working for me. I can honestly say that my year round and summer camp staffs here today are the best I ever had."

He paused for a moment to gather his thoughts. "Some of you I have known since I took over The Park and it has been my pleasure watching you grow up. In a way, it was like having you guys as kids of my own." I had to close my eyes so no one would see them watering up. "And even some of the newer employees. You kept the hardest part of the year easy for me. I'll stop in from time to time to check up on everyone, but I know that if I don't, my park is in good hands. Thank you for many years of memories." We raised our glasses and bottles in the air. It was a salute to the hard work we have done over the years. A salute to Gene. A salute to The Park.

Year Six

October '05

I was sitting at James and Joanne's apartment at school and I could not believe what the voice on the T.V. had just said.

"Is this really happening?" I asked, turning to James, who was already standing, ready to run outside and yell.

"Fuck yeah!" he said. "This is the greatest moment of my life!"

He's right. This is the greatest moment of my life. The White Sox had just won the World Series. My White Sox. I wanted to scream, cry, get drunk, make love, play ball, and call all my friends all at the same time. "We have to get out of here," I said to James and Joanne. "Let's go to Green Street."

"Sounds good, let me get my camera," James said running into his room.

"This makes up for every time Mrs. Owens has made me want to quit the teaching profession and become an alcoholic," I told Joanne as she led the way out the front door and into the brisk autumn air.

"I'm happy for you," she said. "Maybe this can be your motivation to not give up and finish off the semester with her."

Besides our screams, the five-minute walk was quiet. I had this misconception that the streets would be packed with

Sox fans, but apparently campus was too close to St. Louis to experience that. "You want to just go into a bar?" I asked James.

"Yeah, call Cesar, see if he wants to meet up."

"I thought there would be more people out," Joanne said depressingly.

"Me too," I said.

We continued walking, across Springfield Avenue, and were now only a few blocks from Green Street and the center of campus nightlife.

"Do you hear that?" James said to me.

I listened carefully, but could not tell if I heard an actual faint noise or was just imagining it. "Maybe…what is it?"

"I think I see a crowd up there," Joanne said.

I squinted my eyes and an image, hundreds of feet away, came into focus. Green Street was packed with people. "Oh shit!" I said.

"Let's go!" James sprinted ahead.

The passing seconds revealed a thousand or so Sox fans celebrating as one united mass of humanity. I could feel the ground shaking beneath my feet as we joined the almost rioting crowd in the middle of the Sixth and Green intersection.

"So this is where all the Sox fans were!" James yelled out to me above the crowd.

"I gotta find Cesar!" I said.

Two hours, a few beers with Cesar, fireworks, students climbing light poles, and a fellow student teacher inviting me to light some garbage cans on fire later, I was back in my apartment with Edgar. We had been roommates for three years, and he still refused to come out of his room to hang out. I had my car at school and felt like jumping in and driving home to Chicago. Celebrate the win the way it should be, with my city. But I couldn't. Instead I took off my shoes, shirt, and pants, and hopped into bed. I had to teach in the morning and I couldn't miss one day. The thought of being in the same room with Mrs. Owens brought down my spirit, but nothing could diminish what had just happened. It was the greatest day of my life.

November '05

"What do you think you are doing?" Mrs. Owens demanded of me. My heart started racing and my stomach was shrinking in on itself. Three months I had spent student teaching in her room and she still hated me.

"Oh," I said dropping the Skittles. "I thought I could have some." I didn't get it. *Yesterday she offered me candy and today I take one bag and she is mad? Did I miss something here?*

"You can't just take without asking," she responded. "I'm sure you understand that concept." *She wants to kill me, I'm sure of it.*

I was hoping my phone would ring so I could just leave. Another bad day but at least I wouldn't be killed. I tried to think of a good comeback, something that would shut her up but not make me out to be the bad guy. "I'm sorry." *Pussy.*

I continued grading the math worksheets I assigned earlier. I looked up at the clock, 3:32. *Where is Kerri? She is always here by three thirty. Maybe she called and my phone didn't vibrate.* I checked my gray Nokia to be sure. Good reception, but no missed calls. I turned back to my grading, writing a seventy percent on the top of the worksheet in front of me and flipping to the next one. *How does twenty plus five, and twenty plus fifteen, both equal thirty?* It's frustrating when kids can get the hard questions right but cannot use common sense to get the easy ones. I flipped to the next worksheet. My eyes moved from problem to problem looking for mistakes. None as usual for Janessa. I felt so proud. My phone started to vibrate in my pocket. I was free.

I jumped into Kerri's car and felt infinitely better. Just driving away from that bitch everyday was so comforting.

Maybe my mind thought there was a small chance I wouldn't ever see her again. A farming accident perhaps.

Our conversation started off the same way as every other, "How was your day?" Kerri asked.

"Sucked, man. Yesterday she offered me this box of candy and told me I could eat however much I wanted. She told me it was Halloween leftovers. So today at three thirty I am grading papers and she is on her computer and I reach for some Skittles and she yelled at me."

"What the hell? What did she say?" she asked. I swear Kerri hated her as much as I did.

"She told me that I need to ask before I just take them. Even though she just told me yesterday it was okay to eat as much as I wanted. It's not like I was eating in front of the kids. They've been gone since three." I wanted every other U of I student teacher to be placed with Mrs. Owens so they could understand that I wasn't crazy. "She is fucked up."

"Yeah she is," Kerri reinforced, "this is worse than when *she* was teaching and yelled at *you* to keep the kids quiet." I didn't want to think about that day ever again either. "Didn't she tell you that when you are teaching, it is your responsibility to completely run the class?"

"Yeah. She said she didn't want to baby me because in the real world it will only be the students and me. I won't have an experienced teacher to help. But I liked that, it's good practice," I said.

"She's a fucking nut. How can she tell you to run the class yourself and that she won't help you out when the kids are like out of control, but she yells at you for not helping her," Kerri was on a roll. "Isn't *she* the professional teacher?"

"Supposedly a Golden Apple winner," I said. "I just can't wait till all of this is over."

"I know. One more week till break and then three more after that," she said. I debated in my head if four weeks left with Mrs. Owens was 'almost done' or 'a long way to go.'

"I'm so excited!" Kerri continued, interrupting my train of thought.

"Me too," I said. "I just hope she doesn't kill me before winter break."

My last four weeks with Mrs. Owens were not any better. I never felt like crying more than when I was with her. She made me feel like a bad teacher. Someone unworthy to be in the same room as her and her Golden Apple trophy. I didn't care if she won some award, I knew who she really was, a summoned demon of Hades. My last day with her was such an overwhelming relief. My students wrote me letters about how they would miss me and how much I taught them. It was the only thing that kept my morale from reaching zero. That, and knowing next semester I would be teaching back home in Chicago. Mrs. Owens would be two hundred miles away.

When I returned home for Christmas break I decided to reorganize my entire wardrobe. I wanted to look professional when it came to my next placement, giving my co-op no reason to hate me.

After sorting out sizes and styles for an hour or so, I came to my last shelf. The bottom plank of my wardrobe was filled with simple t-shirts that I never bothered to hang. I grabbed the whole shelf full and set them on the ground, uncovering my shirts from camp. Ten in all, ranging from teal, to dark green, to yellow. I held them in my hands and tried to smell the summers gone by. Even though I could only smell fabric softener, each color brought me back to an age of my life when I looked at the world differently.

There were the teal summers, where I only wanted to have fun and make some money. I looked at camp only as a job, a place where I could spend time with my friends. The teal summers gave way to the dark green middle years, where I learned to embrace my job and the kids. My prime transition years. And finally the yellow summer, last summer, which taught me about keeping my head up even when things got rough. That summer taught me everything I needed to know about surviving Mrs. Owens. I had started out that first teal summer with kids and teaching as just a hobby, and now they were my life.

I was no longer a camp employee, but I still couldn't bring myself to throw away the ten camp shirts that were taking up space in my wardrobe. The number of shirts I owned and did not wear amazed me. Probably over half of my collection was bagged by the end of the process, but the colors teal, dark green, and yellow were still on my shelf. It was my way of hanging on to The Park.

February '06

It was a Tuesday morning and I had just finished parking my car in the school's lot for student teaching clinical number two. I was going to get another awful co-op. The kids were going to be too much for me to handle. Everything I learned from camp, my classes, and my other teaching experiences had been erased. I had amnesia.

I arrived an hour early to discuss my responsibilities with my new co-op. We had met once in December; Mrs. Prince left a good first impression. Then again, Fidel Castro would have been an improvement over my last co-op. I walked into the school and headed for the main office to sign in. I told the secretary who I was, and she told me that someone would be around in a minute to show me to my room.

A friendly looking black woman, which was the typical adult profile around the school, came inside the office and searched the classroom mailboxes for anything she may have needed. I looked back down at my feet, thinking about what I was going to say to the class on my first day when I heard a voice. "Hey there." I looked up at the woman from the mail-boxes. "Are you Vince?"

"Oh, yeah," I said confused. I knew this wasn't Mrs. Prince, so why did she know my name?

"Hey, I'm Ms. Black. I'm the aid in Mrs. Prince's room," she cleared up the confusion. "You can come up with me."

"Oh okay." I left the bench in the office and followed her into the hall.

"Every class in the building has an aid," she started to explain as we began ascending the central staircase. "I'm in the room everyday, all day."

"That must be nice," I said, thinking ahead and realizing that having an extra teacher would make things easier come full takeover. We made it up to the third floor classroom without speaking further.

"Come in," she said as I checked my shirt to make sure it was tucked in nicely.

"Hey Mr. Tipre!" I heard before I could find the source of the voice. Then I spotted Mrs. Prince at her desk in the back, just as I remembered from my visit.

"Hi Mrs. Prince." She stood up and came over to shake my hand. With heels she stood probably five foot eight with long black curly hair. She was an attractive black woman in her late twenties or early thirties I guessed. I was getting a good vibe from her. I think she understood what it was like to be in my position. A teacher in training. Scared, yet enthusiastic. Humble, yet cocky. "How are you?"

"Me? No complaints, and yourself?" she asked.

"I'm good, a little nervous to be honest." I began taking off my coat.

She must have seen my state of confusion, as if I was asking, "What do I do next?"

"You can hang your coat in the closet over by the door. The kids will be here in about an hour, so we have some time to talk." I opened the closet and found a hanger as Ms. Black stepped out into the hall. I closed the door and looked around the classroom, scanning a few essays that were hung on the walls. It was all so new to me that I wondered if I would ever get used to it.

"Now Mr. Tipre, have you student taught before?" Mrs. Prince asked.

I walked over towards her desk where she was filling out some paperwork and took a seat. "I did in the Fall. It was two times a week for the whole semester," I explained.

She looked up from her work and put her attention on me. Mrs. Owens never gave me any respect or attention in four months and already Mrs. Prince was looking me in the eye. "How was it? Where was it?" she asked out of actual interest and not formality.

"It was in Monticello, Illinois, a very rural town. The population was about five thousand and ninety nine percent of the people there were white." Her body language seemed to say "Okay, please continue." "The kids were great and we got along fine, but my co-op and I did not."

"I'm sorry to hear that," she said. "I think I am very easy to get along with so we should be fine. I remember student teaching myself and I know how stressful it can be. I hated having a supervisor from my university and my cooperating teaching constantly critiquing me. It can be a lot of pressure, as I'm sure you know."

"Definitely." I was beginning to feel a great weight being lifted off my shoulders. I could tell this experience would be more beneficial. "Is there a place I should sit?"

"All of the back desks are empty, so you can set yourself up there today and move around to wherever you feel comfortable as time goes by. I am only here to help you, Mr. Tipre. I want you to know that when you are done observing me for the first few weeks and take over the classroom yourself, I will not interfere." She walked over to the whiteboard and started erasing old assignments. "This will be your class. As long as you teach each subject at a fifth grade level, the material and style are up to you." She wrote today's date on the board in green. Her long fingernails seemed to wrap themselves around the marker. "I'm sure you know that this school is one hundred percent black. There are several white teachers, but I think only one or two of them are males."

"That's fine. I'm from Chicago so it won't be a problem or anything." I didn't know if I had phrased that exactly the way I intended to.

"These kids are tough though. They come from hard backgrounds. Most of them live here in the public housing buildings and do not have the best family lives, if any." I knew she was just trying to prepare me for the worst. Ms. Black walked back into the room before Mrs. Prince could continue. "Hey girl," she said to her. "I told you Mr. Tipre would be here until May right?"

"Yeah," Ms. Black said. "Are you excited?"

"Definitely." In comparison I could see that she looked around the same age as Mrs. Prince, but much more motherly. Mrs. Prince was someone who I could see bumping into at a bar downtown on the weekend. Not Ms. Black. I could never go out for drinks with Ms. Black, but I could bake cookies with her, that's for sure.

"I was just telling Mr. Tipre about our wonderful children," Mrs. Prince said with sarcasm. "Ms. Black, tell him how great they are."

"I can tell you this much," she said. "If you survive these kids, you can survive anything." I could tell that everyday was a battle for these two women. I couldn't imagine how the students were going to differ from those at camp. I didn't have campers from neighborhoods as bad as these, but they certainly weren't angels like those from Monticello. However difficult the next four months would be, at least I knew I wasn't going to be struggling alone.

"I'm going to try my best," I told her.

"That's all we ask," Mrs. Prince said.

April '06

In my last week of full takeover in Mrs. Prince's class, I was using every skill I had ever learned to deal with my students. The majority of them did not work. I felt bad about doing it, but most of the time I had to teach for those who wanted to learn and not concentrate on those who didn't. Too often I was getting frustrated when a group of students would be talking during a discussion. Ms. Black helped me understand that by waiting on those students to be quiet I was taking away from the students who did care. She also showed me that students who grow up in tough living conditions would have good and bad weeks. The best I could do was make sure I was prepared to teach them everyday. The rest was up to them.

The day before spring break was test day in class. Two of the main units I was teaching had come to a close and I wanted to assess how much the students had learned. I spaced out my social studies westward expansion test and my math probability test, one in the morning and one at the end of the day. I collected the math tests as the bell rang for the kids to go home. "Have a good break," I hollered as they made their way down the stairs toward the exit. Screams of "You too, Mr. Tipre!" made their way back to my ears.

I went back into the class and sat down at a desk in the back. I decided to grade the two tests now before I went home for break.

Mrs. Prince was wiping down the board and Ms. Black was getting water out in the hall. "Does it feel good to be done?" Mrs. Prince asked as she made her way back to her desk. "I know I was enjoying my month of doing nothing."

"Yeah," I answered. "Now I can finish up my portfolio for class. I have to find some more teaching artifacts and write responses to prove I am becoming a better teacher." I paused for a moment to think and then continued, "I will miss having full control though. Well, not really control, that's not possible in this room, but being in charge. It's good practice for my own classroom."

"Well you can always teach the afternoons and I'll teach the mornings," Mrs. Prince suggested. "In fact Mr. Tipre, you can teach as much as you want. I hate math and social studies anyway, so you can keep teaching them whenever you want."

I was pondering the pros and cons of continuing to teach half of the day, getting extra experience versus relaxing during my final weeks before graduation. "Sounds good to me," I decided. "I'll let you know if I am overwhelmed with class work and can't."

"Okay. Remember, you don't have to keep the afternoons, it's just if you want to," she reminded. I enjoyed the fact that she was giving me options instead of telling me what to do. Mrs. Owens would be freaking out if she knew there were teachers in the world that cared about the schedules of their student teachers. "Why don't you get out of here? Finish up those tests over break."

"You sure I can leave now?" I asked.

"Hey, I'm in charge, aren't I?" she joked. "Now go home. Have a good break."

I put my work into my bag and grabbed my coat. "Bye Mrs. Prince. Have a good break."

"You too Mr. T."

I saw Ms. Black in the hallway and wished her a great break as well. I was having mixed feelings. Last semester I couldn't wait for break and now I wouldn't mind having to teach next week. *What a difference six months make.*

Living in Chicago I had a later spring break than my college friends. As I registered for summer school, I knew I needed an act of God to get the classes I needed and somehow still have time to work at The Park, but I was going to try. Right off the bat I signed up for two online classes that were not going to affect my summer. The last two classes were not available online and I hoped I could get into the early summer session classes to be done by mid June, before camp began. My final psychology class was open for the beginning of summer, but my one last class, a biology lab, was only offered in the middle of the summer and ran right through camp. My luck had run out, but I had no choice: I registered for it anyway.

Instead of dwelling in self-pity, I made the best of my break. The White Sox were starting their season long defense of their World Series championship and I did not want to miss a game. The team looked even stronger than last year, if that was even possible, and many experts were predicting an early repeat.

In the time between games I graded my tests and rearranged the class store I was running with Mrs. Prince and Ms. Black. Some of my early ideas were unraveling and the entire foundation of the rewards system needed to be retooled. I also decided that I would go out and buy some really great prizes for the store, so the students had more than Flamin' Hot Cheetos to choose from.

When break ended, I had come to terms with not being able to work at The Park. I gave Mrs. Prince back her mornings and literacy time, and continued working on social studies and math. I figured after student teaching ended, I would just finish up at U of I and start looking for a job in the fall. Because I was not receiving my diploma until August, getting hired for a full time position would be nearly impossible. I would have to apply over the summer. I envisioned a fifty-year-old female principal with shoulder length brown hair and a pointed nose looking at my resume only to see that I wasn't even certified:

"So you want me to hire you?" she would say, looking up from my resume. "But you haven't even graduated. You don't have your diploma or your teaching certificate. Plus, you don't have a letter of recommendation from both your cooperating teachers."

"Well, my first co-op hated me." Defending myself against Mrs. Owens should have been easy. "She disapproved of the way I wanted to teach her students. She told me I had to do it her way or no way."

"She's right. You are a student teacher and have to follow the rules of your co-op's classroom," she would respond, not even looking up this time. Her eyes would widen as she saw some new information. Maybe all of the experience I had with kids prior to student teaching. Maybe it was the fact that my last student teaching experience was in the worst conditions possible and my co-op gave me great ratings.

Finally she would look up and say, "It says here you almost got fired your first year working for the Chicago Park District. You conducted corporal punishment on nine and ten year olds. Made them do pushups and even went as far as putting one kid in the bathroom while another kid had a bowel movement. They are probably scarred for life! It appears you are not suited to work with children on any level." She would hand me back my resume. "Our meeting is over, thank you for wasting my time."

I came home from student teaching on Wednesday and checked my email. My inbox showed one message from my summer school biology professor. I clicked on the link and waited for it to load, figuring it was an introduction to the course.

The email loaded and I began to read. "Attention students enrolled in Molecular and Cellular Biology 103. I am sorry to be informing you after you have registered, but this class will only meet once a week for lab." The information put a smile on my face. I immediately thought of camp...maybe I *could* work. I read on, "I repeat: All lectures are cancelled for my summer session. You have to do the readings on your own and apply the information to your lab work. Email me with any questions."

I emailed him to clarify my situation and he told me that as long as I was at U of I every Tuesday at three o'clock for my lab and tests, I was fine. I called Caitlin and told her the good news. She immediately went with me over to The Park to talk with Kevin. The new supervisor, Eileen, was working instead. I assumed she was going to be running camp now, so I presented my situation to her.

I knew she didn't know me, except for maybe glancing over my name on last year's rec. leader list. I informed her of my work history with The Park and my current dilemma. "I will only have class one day a week. Tuesdays I would need to leave at noon, but other than that, I can be here the rest of the week." I know Gene would have agreed in a second, but I no longer had the privilege of having him as my boss.

Eileen was thinking about my arrangement. I wished Kevin was working so he could support me. Help convince her that I was an important asset to The Park. Caitlin put her hand on my back as if to say "good luck." After what felt like two minutes but was probably only fifteen seconds, Eileen finally said, "I can do this. Make you in charge of play camp. They meet Monday, Wednesday, and Friday mornings. The rest of the time you can work in day camp. That is the only way that *my* boss won't wonder where you are every Tuesday. It won't matter because there is no play camp Tuesdays."

"Hmm, what about Ashley?" I asked. "She ran play camp for the last couple of years."

"Ashley didn't sign up this year," she informed me. "That's why the opening is there for you."

I did not like the sound of her idea one bit. *Play Camp*? I pleaded my case to her, how I didn't understand how some people could miss a weeks worth of camp each year and I only wanted to miss twenty-one hours. Three days total. Why was I going to get punished but no one else ever did? Still, she didn't budge. "Take it or leave it," she told me.

"I'll take it," I said. I was probably making a bigger deal out of it than I should have been. Eileen really was doing me a favor.

"You better go get your drug test taken care of," she reminded me.

"Okay, I'll make an appointment," I signaled that I was leaving to Caitlin. "Thanks Eileen."

We walked out of the field house and down the front steps. "Play camp will be okay," Caitlin reassured me. "It does kinda suck that you'll be in the Women's Building when you're with them, but it's better than not having a job at all."

I thought about her words and knew she was right. It would still be a good year at The Park. Even though I wanted to work with older kids, play camp and its four and five year olds would add to my resume.

In the car I told Caitlin how I did not want to leave Mrs. Prince's class. For three months I got a chance to work with teachers who seemed like real people to me. They cared about each other, they cared about me. I felt at home.

May '06

What happened during my final week of student teaching will stay with me forever. I was grading papers in the back of my class, oblivious to the actions around me. The security guard on our floor was lecturing the students about their misbehavior in the halls. *Mrs. Prince is in charge of the class again, so this is her problem.* As I checked over the last of my students' work, a commotion started across the room. I had heard the security guard raise his voice, but I shrugged it off as another typical warning at my school. Even I was sick of the endless verbal warnings, but I never wanted the guard to lose control. Before I could react, the guard's belt was off and he had bent T, a particularly tough boy in my class, over a chair. He raised the belt above his head.

This must be some sick joke.

A brutal scream left T's lungs empty as the belt struck his back. Instincts took over and I panicked. I looked for my cooperating teacher to speak up, but she remained silent and unmoved by the scene. *WHAT THE FUCK IS GOING ON?* The screams of the second and third hits were too loud to be unanswered, but a small group of teachers and parents that were now gathered by the door ignored them. I saw the watery eyes of some of the girls, and the fear stricken stares of the boys. My grading marker rolled off my desk as I rose from my chair and headed past the group of adults and out into the hall.

"Good, he probably deserved it," I heard the mother say as the fourth hit landed violently across T's back.

Deserved it? Does anyone deserve this, let alone a helpless eleven year old? The hallway was uncharacteristically quiet. I wondered if everyone could hear T's horrifying screams. I had the urge to walk back in the room and beat the shit out of the security guard. I don't doubt I would have if he was not six five and two hundred eighty pounds. He was as intimidating to me as he was to the scared boys in the class. I guess he thought the beating would scare some respect into the class.

Another hit, another scream. *Will this ever end?* I feared that T's life was being taken from him, physically and emotionally. Everything was backward. He was the security guard, he should have been protecting the kids, not lashing them. I was supposed to be feeling excited, not terrified, during my last week. The teachers on the floor should have been taking action, helping T, stopping the screams, but they just stood, like an audience at a comedy club. To them, the live action was more important than the consequences. It was as if the teachers and parents were cheering for the temporary silencing of the classroom over a child's entire future. I made excuses for them. They were intimidated like me. Perhaps I had walked out of the room when they were seconds away from calling the police. Maybe I was dreaming…a nightmare. I saw Ms. G, a fourth grade teacher, sitting alone in her class. I walked inside, looking to escape the sound of the belt whipping and T's wails.

"What's that sound?" she asked.

It was two P.M. on my second to last day, and T's screams were filling the third floor. Two days left of student teaching and I was supposed to be concentrating on two things. Putting the finishing touches on my portfolio and testing my students on planet Earth. The latter was coupled with a *Jeopardy!* style review for Tuesday morning so the students would gain some confidence before the test. I would be Alex Trebek and they would be Ken Jennings. This way we could knock out the work before we celebrated my farewell in the afternoon. I should have been focusing on my class party, on graduation, on the beginning of summer. But, all I could think about was the screaming.

"The security guard is hitting T with his belt," I told her the truth.

"What?" A young teacher, like myself, she was in complete shock by the situation. "That's him screaming?"

"Yeah."

"Oh my god." She wanted to cry, to take action, to yell "STOP," but she was paralyzed by the situation, confused and helpless. I tried to think of a solution. *Run downstairs and get the principal. Call the police. Walk up to the security guard, grab his arm, force the belt from him, and make him wish he was never born.* Instead, I froze. Another hit landed, and now over a hundred feet away, I heard no scream, just silence. Someone walked past Ms. G's room and I caught a glimpse of the security guard. Like an executioner after a beheading, his job was done. A hired hitman, an assassin. I walked back across the hall with courage I wished I had minutes before. The class was silent, the parents and teachers dispersing. T laid crumpled over in the back, his body shaking from the hits, exhausted from the screams. Not one student made eye contact with me, like they were ashamed. *I have let them down when they needed me the most.*

I went home that night and relived the experience over and over again as I told my family what happened. My brothers and I discussed the morality of the situation. They explained that I needed to do what I felt was right, even if that meant I placed the teachers who were present under criticism. I emailed my principal, telling her that I needed to talk to her in the morning about an incident that happened at school. I tried to not give anything away because I was not sure how to tell her. That night I thought over the situation as I laid in bed, struggling to find a perfect solution: one where I knew I had done everything I could to help T and punish the security guard, while at the same time not making it look like I am undermining the certified teachers I have established a semester long relationship with. Every choice led to someone getting upset with me. Each path was filled with possible repercussions. I finally fell asleep at two A.M., without a clue as to how I was going to handle the situation in the morning.

When I woke up, the answer was as clear as day. I would go straight to the principal and tell her the exact truth. If I wanted to take my future as an educator seriously, I needed to start now. I hopped in the shower, brushed my teeth, grabbed a banana for breakfast, and headed out the door. In the car ride I noticed my pride slightly overpowering the nervous sensation in my gut. When I walked into the school, I knew I was doing the right thing. I was not sticking up for just T, but for all the kids, their futures, and myself.

"Come in," the principal called me in her office. I took a seat across from her. A large wooden desk separated us, piled high with stacks of papers and books. *A buffer zone, just in case what I tell her turns her into the Hulk.*

"So Mr. Tipre, I want you to explain everything to me," she began.

I sat up in my chair and gathered my thoughts. I knew that misrepresenting what happened could have serious consequences. "Some of the boys were acting up in the hallway yesterday after library, so the security guard on our floor decided to pay a visit to the class to talk about hallway behavior." As I talked, my words started to feel almost judicial. I was speaking the truth and could do no wrong. The principal did not break eye contact with me the entire time I spoke. She responded with only head nods, letting me finish the retelling without interruption.

When I finished there was a lingering silence. "Thank you for letting me know. I will contact the proper authorities and keep you updated on the situation," she finally said.

"I'm sorry I didn't tell you yesterday," I said.

"In the future, don't hesitate with something this important, but at least you came forward." She wrote something down on a sheet of paper. I stood up and began to leave. "I know this is your last full day. I will visit your room before the day is over," she promised.

"Okay."

A great sense of relief swept over me. I knew that I did my part and could only hope the principal followed through on the report. I walked up the three flights of stairs to my room, barely remembering that I had a *Jeopardy!* review to setup.

T showed up for class and most of the kids seemed scared to talk to him. They probably didn't know what to say. I didn't know what to say either. Nevertheless, the day went by smoothly and I almost forgot about the incident amidst the music, pizza and soda at my going away party.

That night I finished cards I had been writing to each of my students. They were mostly notes of encouragement and thanks. I saved T's note for last. I thought about what I could say that would make the situation better. To make his entire life better. I wanted to be able to cure him of all the pain he had felt in his life, erase his memories, push reset, but I knew I couldn't. I decided the best I could do was tell him I believe in him. Tell him that I will miss all the talks about Kobe Bryant and Michael Jordan. Let him know that he did nothing to deserve the things that had happened to him. That it is up to him to get away from the life that he told me so many times he hated. I wished him luck and told him to keep his hopes up, even when so many people are trying to bring them down. I cried as I signed the card because I knew his chances, like so many of my other students, were not all that great. Life doesn't always help those in need, and too often, just when you think you have made it, life painfully reminds you that you haven't.

As I drove home after my last day, I thought back on how far I had come. The students were anything but angels, and even the good ones would have been the most disruptive in Mrs. Owens's class, but I connected with them. I was able to see inside the lives of thirty fifth graders and had an impact on them. I knew I changed some of the students. Others I only hoped to have reached. One thing was definite, *I* changed.

I was not afraid anymore, not scared of students, or campers, or principals. I wanted to break the rules and change the system. I saw what education could do for the most neglected children. It gave them an escape. Hope. Opportunity. Someone needed to set them on the right path to achieve it. I was determined to be that someone.

June '06

I participated in the May graduation ceremony and moved back down to U of I for one month of summer school. Derek was in Arizona finishing up his degree during the summer and definitely not working at The Park. Nick even quit his job as a year round park employee because his family moved out to the suburbs. It wasn't worth the forty-minute drive into work everyday. He still deliberated coming back for the six weeks of camp, but when he got a new job out by his house, he jumped at the opportunity at year round work.

Cesar had moved on from The Park as well. I had spent most of my years running the oldest boys group with him by my side, and now he would be a thousand miles away when camp started. He was hired for his dream job, working for the Cincinnati Reds Rookie Ball team in Florida as an athletic trainer. When we talked on the phone he told me he was happy to have a job in baseball, but still wasn't completely satisfied.

"You're right man," I said sarcastically. "Traveling with the team, watching baseball all day, meeting future big leaguers, it must be rough."

"Yeah, it is a pretty sweet gig. I just hope soon it will be for the White Sox," he elaborated. "I feel like a traitor working for the National League." It was comforting to know that some people never change.

I don't know how she was up to it, but Cristina was working again after giving birth a month before camp started. It made me feel old knowing that someone I worked with for years, who was my age, was already a parent. It also made me realize how much everyone must love camp. Even childbirth can't stop The Park. When all the dust settled, James, Cristina, and I were the only rec. leaders remaining from my first year.

Not only had the employee roster gone through many changes, but we now had a new boss. Eileen was the new park supervisor, but she would not be in charge of camp. That responsibility was left to New Julie.

New Julie was the polar opposite of Old Julie. She was thin, strange, close-minded, and ran a confusing camp. Kevin was still in charge of play camp, composed of four and five year old boys and girls housed in the Women's Building. It existed as a whole other world apart from day camp. Luckily it was only twelve hours a week, so I still had my older boys' group when play camp ended. New Julie paired me with James for my time with day camp. We had not worked together in four years and I could not wait for our reunion.

James was now a certified middle and high school teacher while I was two months shy of getting my certification in elementary education. The two of us had a combined eleven years of rec. leading experience and nine years of college coursework under our belts. We both student taught the previous year, and even ran after school programs for grade school kids down in Champaign. We were probably the most qualified rec. leaders in the history of the world. We were ready for anything our group could throw at us.

We weren't ready for New Julie changing the camp schedule around on us. The simple routine we followed every year was golden. There were never any problems and all the groups had their fair share of time in the pool, playground, and fields. New Julie wanted us to "rotate" around a set activity each day. The first day of camp we were all given set gym times, and the rest of our day would revolve around those. No one followed her lead because no one could understand it.

To make things worse, our schedule changed on day two. "Today we are going to rotate around art," New Julie said. "Make sure you pay attention to your schedules so you don't end up in the same place as someone else." She seemed so proud.

Cristina raised her hand. "I don't have gym on my schedule today."

"And my group has the art room at the same time as Grace's," Dale added.

New Julie fired back at Cristina, "That's okay, the girls don't need gym everyday." She didn't even acknowledge Dale's problem, which made Dale's jaw drop and the rest of us laugh. She was incompetent, we all knew it, so how did she get hired?

"My group swims at the end of the day now," Jaimie said. "Yesterday we swam in the morning. My parents are not going to know where to find their kids."

New Julie looked at Jaimie like her point was completely worthless. "Kids get tired of having the same schedule every-day. I'm putting in the extra work to shake things up." A smile formed on her face as she looked around for any more questions. James raised his hand with vehemence. "Yes, James?"

I knew he was going to eat her alive. He knew The Park inside and out and was the last person to back down from a chance to humiliate someone.

"The kids are going to hate this," he started. "Camp needs structure. The kids need structure. This does not give it to them. Why can't we stick with our old schedules? They worked perfectly every year." *Not as bad as I thought. Maybe student teaching taught him a thing or two.*

"Let's try this out, I think it will work," New Julie responded. Everyone was too frustrated to argue. We were going to make sure all of the complaints went straight to her. I was sure there would be at least ten a day, maybe more. James and I went upstairs to meet with our campers.

An hour later New Julie was gone. I didn't know if the morning meeting had any effect on her, but she apparently got into an argument with Eileen and Kevin and bolted. I figured she would call in sick or show up the next day without her pride. The next day turned into next week. Next week turned into never. Kevin told me that New Julie was emotionally unstable and was only working at Independence because she was demoted from her previous position. She tried to tell Eileen how to run her park, but Eileen is a badass. She knocked out New Julie eight hours into the camp year. Put that bitch in her place. Eileen may not be the three hundred pound intimidating force like Gene, but she will fuck you up.

The oldest boys group was the best it had ever been. Mikey and Peter were again the two best kids in the group, but this year they had competition. Eccentric Michael from James's group last year was back with his behavior still wild and uncontrollable. He seemed to fuel the rest of the group. I swear that his constant yelling and random chewing on his hand kept everyone on edge and pumping with adrenaline. Camp also went international, with Italian citizen Nicola in our group. He was visiting his relatives for the summer and didn't speak a lick of English, but man could he kick a soccer ball.

Mikey and Peter were Independence Park day campers just like James and I were. They were here year after year, and invested more than just six hours a day into The Park. We knew how much camp meant to them, so James and I did everything we could to make their time memorable. Not since Butthole did we have campers who were more like friends.

We signed kids in and out in the gym now, so rather than playing catch every afternoon outside, the four of us would talk about video games. We shared opinions about the best characters in *Super Smash Bros. Melee*, and the better system maker, Microsoft or Sony. Our discussions almost led to an afternoon of Nintendo playing. Too bad Mikey and Peter were twelve and their parents did not support our play date.

Unfortunately I was limited to half days with my new friends. Play camp was my morning duty, and it was a definite change compared to the older boys. Most of the time I felt more like a babysitter than a rec. leader, a position I never would have signed up for willingly. But, after a few hours, it was time to say goodbye to my young boys and join back up with real camp. I think I had started to take regular day camp for granted after all these years.

The second week of camp meant my first trip down to school for my weekly lab and test. The material was very complicated, but I knew I only had to skate by. I had never received a "C" from U of I but I couldn't care less at this point what my grade was, as long as I passed. I spent all Tuesday morning studying in the gym as the group played 'sit down dodgeball.' Just when I thought I found an answer to the specific type of protein found in larger muscle tissue, Michael came running towards me.

"Tackle Vince!" he screamed like he was possessed.

"Michael stop it," I commanded, trying to fend off his attack while reading the answer to my question.

"Rarrr." His voice was more wild feline, than human.

"James help me!" I shouted across the gym.

"Haha, Michael get him!" *James is the best.*

"Tackle Vince!" This time Michael jumped on my back and began clawing at my neck.

It was time to pull out all the stops. "Winkleman, can you come here and get this kid off of me?" Winkleman was the biggest camper I had ever had, by far. He was only twelve years old, but stood a menacing six feet, and Michael would do absolutely anything he asked of him. And at that point, I didn't care if Michael stopped out of respect or fear.

"Michael, come here," Winkleman's words were like magic. Michael ran back towards the dodgeball game in progress, yelling at the top of his lungs. I think I heard the words "attacked" and "giant man child" amidst his cries.

"Thanks Winkleman," I said, getting back to my studying.

"You're welcome. So, your first test today?" Everyone knew my hectic situation.

"Yeah, I have to leave in about ten minutes, drive down to school, take this test, and complete my lab."

"One time we dissected a frog in science class," Winkleman added proudly.

"Nice," I said, trying to be short with him so he would let me be. He joined the match and Peter hit him the first second he stepped on the court. *That's my boy.*

I went back to studying for a few minutes but couldn't concentrate. The best thing for me was to relieve my stress by blasting some campers with our foam dodge balls. James and I had unwritten rules about hitting each other. Simply put, we didn't. The game was just more fun when we were in it. The first ball I picked up, I looked to hit Nicola. His limited vocabulary spat out the words "Not me, not me." I showed mercy and nailed Michael instead, who then proceeded to chase me around the gym while chewing his hand and screaming something about conspiracies.

"Michael stop, please," Nicola said, which was amazing on two levels. One that he was speaking English, and secondly that he felt the exact same way about Michael as everyone else.

I checked the clock in the gym as I jetted away from Michael one more time. Time for me to hit the road. "James, I'm outta here," I said, running to get my book and notes from the sidelines.

"Good luck man."

I pushed open the back door, feeling the cool breeze from the outside world. "Hey Michael," I yelled. "Tackle James for me, will ya?" The look on James's face turned from cheery to angry in a heartbeat. I closed the door and hurried to my car, but not without first hearing the screams of "Tackle James!" coming from inside.

July '06

When I picked up the *Harry Potter* series a year and a half ago, I thought I had simply found a story that was intriguing enough for me to read. But since last winter I had become lonely without a book in my hand. By the third week of camp, I came home and read everyday. Sox games were no longer my afternoon priority. The *Tales of the Otori* trilogy by Lian Hearn once again filled my fantasy book quota. I had, however, come a long way from when I would only read books about elves, wizards, and mythical worlds. I tackled historical fiction and war epics, romance novels, comedies, mysteries, and even philosophy, which since high school had never had a very high standing in my heart. I admired the way I could get so involved in one book, finish it, and fall in love with a new story the next day. I was like a sixteen-year-old boy all over again, but instead of lusting for mini skirts, I yearned for paperbacks.

Still, nothing reeled me in like fantasy novels. Since my childhood, when I grew up watching *Star Wars* everyday, I had been unable to shake the need to be taken away into worlds so different than my own. I knew I would not be content in my life without those places. The movies, books, and stories that would forever capture my mind were a part of me. A defining characteristic even. Some of my former girlfriends did not understand this, which is a possible reason I never had a stable relationship until now.

Caitlin understood.

Over the summer, there was always one of the *Harry Potter* movies in her DVD player. While I had a limit to the amount of Harry I could handle, she seemed to have an endless infatuation with him. It was a Friday night when I finished the last Otori book in the trilogy. I put the book back on my shelf, admired my recent accomplishment, and pulled out my phone to return a call I missed from Caitlin earlier.

"Hey, sorry I missed your call, I was finishing up my book."

"So the book is more important than me? What if I needed something important? What if I was dying?"

"If it was important you would have kept calling," I retaliated. "Are you dying?"

"Well, what if I wanted you to come over for sex?" Even though the chance of that was very slim, she was right, I should have picked up. Fantasy novels don't really fulfill fantasies. Not unless you're really kinky.

"I'm coming over!" I jokingly exclaimed, still hoping the offer was on the table.

"I was kidding, we're not having sex tonight," she said. Bon Jovi's "Shot Through the Heart" began playing in my head. "Come over, we can watch a movie."

I knew I had nothing to do. After camp I either read or hang out with Caitlin. I saw the guys, usually James and Dale, on weekends when she worked her second job at Petco. "Okay," I told her. "I'm leaving now."

I was at her new basement apartment ten minutes later. Nicole, her sister, and roommate, opened the door for me.

"Good evening," I said to them as I took off my shoes. "Are you making food?"

With her head in the fridge Caitlin responded, "Yeah, I'm hungry. I haven't eaten all day. The lunches were gross today."

"Aren't they always?" Nicole asked her. Everyone knew that camp lunches, just like school lunches, were tasty about once a week. You can tell how bad the situation was when the food industry tried to pass off ketchup packets as a serving of fruit. Apparently even they were too cheap to just give every kid an apple.

"Not always, yesterday it was good. Roast beef I think," Caitlin answered. She closed the fridge door with a sigh and walked over to the couch. "What are we eating?"

"La Villa?" Nicole suggested.

"I'll order," I said.

When I finished ordering our pizza I spotted Caitlin looking through her DVDs. She acted like there was some decision to be made, but we all knew what she would pick. Out of her twenty movies, half of them were *Star Wars*, *Lord of the Rings*, and *Harry Potter* movies, and the other half Adam Sandler comedies. "*Goblet of Fire* or *Return of the King*?" she asked.

"*Return of the King*," Nicole, the bigger *Lord of the Rings* fan, answered. The ying to Caitlin's *Harry Potter* yang.

She put in the movie and the three of us sat down in their new living room on a Friday night in the middle of summer with a pizza on the way. *This is bliss.*

Camp was filled with a routine schedule over the years. Even with a new supervisor and camp director, most of the rec. leaders continued traditions Old Julie taught us. My favorite tradition of the camp year was Scavenger Hunt Day. James and I always expanded a predetermined list, consisting of tasks such as, 'bring us five cartons of milk,' to include find out questions, as in 'who is the oldest camper?'

Instead of the traditional 'bring us something purple,' we spiced it up:

"Bring us a kid covered completely in purple?" Peter was reading one of the questions out loud in disbelief.

"That's right," James said. "Use your imagination."

The scavenger hunt usually lasted thirty minutes, with kids splitting into groups and running amok searching for answers and objects. After asking campers to unravel rec. leader oriented questions over the years, I had mastered writing questions that were fun for both the campers and myself:

1. Bring us ten baseball hats.
2. Find us a penny from 1988.
3. How many water fountains are inside the field house?
4. Which rec. leader lost their entire group four years ago? ("STOLEN FROM ME!" Derek would claim).
5. How much is two cheese dogs, three nachos, and one root beer from the hot dog guy?

Preparing the questions was almost as fun as watching the kids run around with their assignment. If I could make homework this fun I would win a Nobel Prize. James and I camped out in one location and waited for the thirty minutes to pass. Occasionally one of the counselors who was helping a group would come up to us asking for advice.

"Is it okay to check the girls locker room for water fountains?" Carlos asked. He was not our counselor, but being a former camper of mine for years, I made sure to include him every Scavenger Hunt Day.

"Sure," James told him. "Have fun buddy."

"The ladies are going to love my nipples!" he proclaimed as he ran back inside.

James and I reminisced about the previous scavenger hunts, how fast time had gone by, and we even talked about Butthole and Concust, BOK and Big White, Gene and Julie. It seemed like only a few years ago we were the ones in camp, making game winning shots and catching touchdown passes from our rec. leaders. James and I had spent almost every summer at Independence together for the last fifteen years. I couldn't even recall a time before James, before camp, before The Park.

"I don't think I will ever stop working here," I said to James. "There is no reason to ever leave."

"Okay," he said. "I'm completely serious, let's work here until we die."

"We should run camp one day. Teach during the school year and run The Park during summer. We basically do already."

"Sir, we have been running this park since we were twelve," he said. "The rest is just paperwork."

It was kind of true. Rec. leaders never interacted with campers when we were twelve the way we do now. Back then, we ran the show. Most of the time I didn't even know where my rec. leaders were or what we were supposed to be doing. If we wanted to play basketball, we got one out and shot around. If we wanted to go to the playground, we went. Most of the time growing up James and I would hang out with Gene. We would help him carry stuff around and clean up The Park, and in the end, he would reward us with pizza. Good thing he never found out that we accidentally hit his car with coleslaw containers one day. My entire existence could be different.

Thirty minutes was over and the campers returned with their findings. We checked their answers while they changed for swimming.

"Can we do scavenger hunt everyday?" James asked me.

"I will start thinking of new questions as soon as I get home," I replied.

"We could use the same questions tomorrow," James advised as he marked off unanswered questions on some team's sheet. "Only Peter would catch on."

"You're probably right."

Last year it was Game Boys, but year six our campers were into the Yugioh collectable card game. The game was marketed at ten year olds, so I knew Mikey and Peter were capable of a more challenging game. I introduced them to Magic, the original collectable card game. The rules were vastly more complicated but still manageable. Normally athletic campers wanted to play sports. Mikey and Peter were both good athletes, but Magic really spiked their interest. Another lesson for me that sports only had to be a small part of day camp.

Peter was going on a road trip with his older brother the last week of camp so today, Friday, would be his last day. It was time for swimming and James ordered the boys to get their towels and suits. Peter did not want to spend his last hour ever as a camper swimming when he could do that at home. I would like to think that he would have wanted to spend time with me whether or not I brought my Magic cards that day.

James volunteered to watch the group as they swam so Peter, Mikey, and I could play without Eileen throwing a fit. We set up my cards in a room upstairs by the auditorium. I was surprised they remembered so many of the game's concepts and rules from the few times I had demonstrated them. *I must be the greatest teacher ever.* The game functions similar to solitaire, where you pick up cards and lay them out in front of you according to what they do. I remember the lengthy three or so years it took me to really grasp the goals of Magic because my only teacher was Nick, another twelve-year-old beginner. At the table I meshed my knowledge of the game with my tools as a teacher to present the rules in an understandable and thorough manner. Having two students who cared about the material was a bonus.

Peter, Mikey, and I were finishing up our last game when I heard the rest of our group leaving the locker room downstairs. "The boys are done swimming. We have to finish this up."

"Okay, I'll kill you in a couple turns," Peter said smiling. He was a perfect blend of skill and modesty.

It was Mikey's turn and he was doing some thinking. Just last game he made a simple mistake that cost him the game and he was double-checking his plan in his head. "Vince, I attack you with him," he said pointing to his biggest creature, "and Peter I attack you with everything else." A smile formed across his face.

"I can't stop it, so I'm dead," I confessed. I began packing away the cards I used to make the clean up easier. Peter studied the situation in front of him. I wanted to let them make their own decisions, and unavoidable mistakes, and then go back and show them what could have been done differently. Peter fended off the attack without dying, but his life total was very low.

"Are you done?" Peter asked Mikey, eager to see what he could cast on his own turn.

"Oh, yeah, sorry."

Peter proceeded with his turn and during each phase he looked up at me, almost asking, "Am I doing this right?" He used his mana in order to cast Wrath of God. "I use this to kill all creatures." Mikey was not happy. "Then I bring in this Angel with the mana I have left." *Good move.* "Your turn."

Mikey was not able to pick up any useful cards in the next few turns that could finish off Peter, and soon the Angel won him the game. "I told you I was going to win," he said. His modesty went right out the window.

"Well, I killed Vince," Mikey pointed out what he considered the grand prize.

"Yeah yeah," I packed away the rest of the cards and looked at my phone. Camp was already over. "From now on I won't let you win."

"You didn't let us win, you just suck," Mikey shot back.

Maybe he was right, but it still felt good knowing that I had the instinct, from my teaching experiences, to introduce them to the game. Teaching in rural Monticello and then urban Chicago allowed me to see the variety of interests kids could have. Camp was a very short and limited experience, but I was mastering the methods needed to reach my campers on multiple levels.

We walked down the stairs towards our sign out location in the gym. I continued to joke with them, "I gave you guys my good cards, so I had to use a bad deck."

"Yesterday you said that your black deck was your best one," Peter said, catching me in my lie. I did use my black deck and it was my best, and I didn't let them win.

"All luck," I countered.

We joined James and the few remaining campers in the gym. I let James talk to Peter for the time he had left on his last day. Even though I was closer with Peter now, it was James, not me, that was invited to, and attended, his birthday party three years ago. I know that it was extremely nice of James to show up and it probably made Peter's day, but at the time I couldn't imagine how awkward he must have felt being the only one to have hit puberty at the party. Now I wished for the day that Peter had his next birthday party so I could be invited. Once Michael was picked up, the excitement of camp was lost, and Peter decided to leave.

"You better be here next year," James said to him. "You can be my counselor." He was trying to steal away my chance at attending his birthday party.

"Or, you can be my counselor and we can play Magic everyday when the group swims." *Do bribes work on twelve year olds?*

"Bye James," he said, unsure about what to do next. James decided for him and gave him a hug.

Peter hugged me next. I wished him luck in school and told him I would see him next summer. Then he hugged Mikey. Two boys who were only friends for six weeks a year, hugging, in front of two boys who used to be only friends for six weeks a year. *Maybe one day Peter and Mikey will be rec. leaders, and they will have James's kids, or my kids, in their group.* In reality, it was comforting to know that the thought wasn't that farfetched.

Two things happened then, at the end of July, which made me stop and reflect on the time I had spent working at The Park. First, Butthole dropped by for a visit. It was the first time I had seen him in about a year, and the first time I saw him with facial hair. Butthole, my smart mouthed camper, was shaving. *What the fuck, how old am I?* Realistically, it was great knowing that someone who was in my group five years previous still wanted to visit. We talked about the Angels and Airwaves album and his new girlfriend. Never was there hesitation to ask questions, never an awkward moment. Just good conversation on top of the best memories.

A few days after Butthole's appearance, Caitlin and I celebrated our two-year anniversary. *Two years.* I had trouble remembering when Caitlin was just that cute counselor who would chase me around. That night we talked about the past, reliving our first years working at The Park, but truthfully it all seemed like a dream. *A distant time or place.* She asked me if I thought it was weird that we were together.

"Maybe at first, but now it would only be weird if we were *not* together," I told her.

"I still can't believe that you want to be with me," she replied.

In reality, I am the one who got what I always wanted. It just took me a while to see that the person was right in front of me the whole time.

August '06

I took my last trip down to Champaign on the Tuesday of the last week of camp. I had some trouble on my biology lab final, specifically remembering the differences between human and rat reproductive systems, but overall I figured I pulled an "A" or "A-" in the course. My *last* course at U of I ever. I packed up the small remains I had at my old apartment, a vacuum and a mop mostly, and began my last drive home from the cornfields. I could not have been happier. My iPod was plugged in with the volume turned all the way up.

Back at camp on Wednesday, Julia congratulated me the first chance she could. "I can't believe you are done with school!"

"I can't believe it either."

"Don't you feel so old?"

"Well now I do."

She let out a subtle laugh, "Honestly, you give me motivation to get into a good college."

"You should," I encouraged. "You start applying in a couple months right?"

"Yeah. I'm probably going to go to school for teaching."

"What happened to being a chef?"

"I can do both," she said. "Hey, maybe I will teach people how to cook."

"Can you teach Caitlin?"

"Wow, I'm going to tell her you said that."

"No don't, I was kidding."

"Okay, okay."

"No seriously, teach her."

I was so relieved to be done. Julia really put my accomplishment in perspective. In a few weeks, I would receive my diploma and teaching certificate in the mail. *Me, a certified teacher. Who would pay me to watch their children?* The school year would start up soon and I wanted to be available to sub the first week. Life was turning out better than I had ever imagined.

The final three days of camp were completely carefree. No more studying during gym time, no more online quizzes on Friday nights. I could enjoy the rest of my summer.

Eileen rewarded my group with pizza during the last Thursday of camp. Even though she gave each group pizza one time during the year, I was holding the idea of hot cheese and crunchy crust over their heads for most of the summer. We ate our slices on paper plates and used the milk from the box lunches to wash them down. When the boxes were empty and our stomachs full, I went around and gathered the cardboard disks from the pizza boxes.

I made a pile of pizza disks on the ground, and Mikey and I started playing catch with one as if it was a Frisbee. He tried to throw it to me, but it was taken by the wind and landed in the middle of a group of my boys who were finishing their food.

"Wow, meanest guys of all time!" James hollered at me. He picked up the cardboard and flung it back to me. I snatched his out of the air and grabbed a second from the ground. Both flew across the sky. How they headed in opposite directions, when I threw them the same way, is beyond me. Mikey launched one to James and soon a few more campers wanted in on the action. Within a minute there were a dozen or so pizza disks filling the sky, including one that hit me in the face.

"That's it! No one is swimming!" I screamed jokingly.

"Alright!" Nicola replied.

Tomorrow would be the last day of camp and the talent show. Today was just another day of lighthearted fun. *I wouldn't have it any other way.*

I was never much of a performer, even in front of a child-filled audience, but some days I just felt like dressing up as a woman. *Natural Woman* by Aretha Franklin blared through the speakers during the talent show. The last song capping our ode to women. The applause was overwhelming when I stepped onto the stage. I couldn't tell if it was for my stubble or short skirt. I danced with my boys just like we rehearsed. When it came time to grab a partner, I eyed James who was sitting right in front. I dragged him on stage and we slow danced to a crowd full of laughter.

"This is the life," I told him, admiring how well our show was going.

He looked at me and could not help but laugh. "You are one hideous woman, you know that right?"

"You love it," I said. When our cue came, my boys and I lined up to take our final bows. I could see several people in the audience pointing at me. I envisioned my boxers riding up during the show and revealing everything. "Let's go," I said to the boys around me, frightened that my thoughts became reality.

We trotted down into the art room and began to celebrate another successful talent show performance. Some of the boys were not that eager to take off their two-piece bathing suits and tube tops. James popped in shortly after.

"Hey there," I said to him. "Did you happen to see any of my, well manhood, when I was dancing?"

"Haha, trust me, I looked," he joked, "but you were all covered so don't worry."

"I was worried," I said, glad that James had removed the six-inch weight that was sitting upon my shoulders.

"Tackle Vince!" Michael hollered from behind me. He jumped for my shoulders but the dress he was wearing made it nearly impossible to move.

"You have to take off your dress if you want to tackle me buddy," I said to him.

"If no one claims this skirt can I keep it?" Winkleman asked me as he restrained Michael with his outstretched arm.

"Listen guys, I know you want to keep the outfits," I said to them, "but they are not yours." I began to take off my outfit and put my pants and shirt back on. "Let's go Winkelman. Those pantyhose need to be returned."

"Aw, no one will know I took em," he pleaded with me. "Please?"

I gave him a harsh look and he immediately took them off. I always thought that kid was unique. I wondered if he had figured it out yet himself.

After James and I gathered all of the outfits and accessories, we brought the group upstairs to sign out. A mob of parents who were at the show were already waiting. The last day was always like this. All you wanted to do was hang out a little longer with these kids, and before you knew it, they were all gone. Some would be seen next summer, most never again.

Michael's dad was next in line to sign out, so James brought over the costume bag their family had supplied. "Hey Vince, hey James, nice show," his dad congratulated us.

"Thanks, you'd be surprised how many boys went from hating the idea of being girls to loving it," James educated him.

"Actually, I see Michael at home, practicing and trying on his mother's outfits, and I believe it." He grabbed the pen from me and found his son's name on the list. "Come on Michael," he said to his fast approaching son.

"TACKLE VINCE!" Michael bellowed one last time. When the summer started I avoided his spontaneous tackles, but now I looked forward to them. I let him jump on my back and we crashed into the padded gym walls. But not being sure of his father's reaction, I quickly brought him back to the clipboard and he hopped off.

"That was so much fun," Michael said to me, breathing heavily. "Next year we have to remember that one!"

"Sounds good to me," I said as Michael gave James a high five. "Have a good school year."

"You too guys," Michael's dad responded, his son already out the gym door.

There was no time to linger on that goodbye because Winkleman was finally out of costume and ready to sign himself out and walk home. "Aw man Winkleman," James said when he grabbed the clipboard. "I already miss seeing you dressed like Winklewoman."

"Really?" his voice sounded shocked. "I can put my outfit back on."

"That's alright kid," James said, "why don't you come back and work here next year?"

Winkleman put down the pen and focused on James's words. "Be a counselor? How do I sign up?"

"Come with me," I said. I looked at James as Winkleman grabbed his bag, "I'm going to take him to talk to Eileen."

"Sounds good," James said, handing the clipboard to the next parent in line.

Winkleman and I walked into the office and Eileen was surprisingly not busy. "First time I have ever seen you without a pile of work to do," I said.

"There's work, I'm just overseeing this last camp sign out right now," she responded. "So what did he do?" her gaze now on Winkleman.

"Nothing, I wanted to have you put down his name on your counselor list for next year," I told her. She pulled out a sheet of paper and asked for his name.

"When do I have to come and sign up?" Winkleman asked. I was proud of him taking initiative.

"I would say come in the beginning of April," she informed him.

"Thanks Eileen, come on Winkleman." The two of us left the office and paused in the hallway. The park house was quiet. It was not even three o'clock and yet it seemed like camp was over for hours. "So don't forget about April," I reminded him.

"Yeah I know, I won't," he said. Then he turned and walked out the back doors toward the field, not to be seen for another year. By the time I got back into the gym, the chaos that was our costumes, kids, and parents scattered all over was down to a simple few. I rejoined Mikey, James, and the others, who were preparing for a game of hacky sac.

"So is Winkleman all set for next year?" James asked me, picking up the dropped sac from the floor.

"As long as he shows up in April to register."

"Another year…another year," James said quietly.

We played for a few minutes but the game died out when two more parents came. Mikey hung around even after the rest of the group was gone. I started to feel the same way I had about Butthole three years before. Not wanting to say goodbye, not wanting to wait ten more months to see this kid, my friend, again. "So, are you going to be a counselor next year?" I asked him.

"Of course," he said. "My sister already is, so she is going to make me come with her when she signs up."

"Good. But you can't leave it up to her. Go home today and write it on your calendar or something. Signup is usually around April or May."

"Okay I will," he said. "Are you going to come back next year?"

"What if I don't?" I asked him.

"Well I would still sign up, but it would be cool if you were working again. I could be your counselor." His sister came over and told him it was time to leave. "I love camp," he said to me. "I'll be here every summer."

"I know exactly how you feel," I told him. "See you next year."

"See you Vince."

I smiled.

Epilogue

D erek returned home from Arizona at the end of August. He unpacked the life he had lived for the last four years and started fresh back in Chicago. He had asked James to take some pictures for him at camp because this summer was the first time he was not at camp in six years. James did one better. Derek had all but forgotten about his request to James, but that first night back, we all gathered around the T.V. in my basement.

"Derek, I don't know if you remember this, but in the beginning of the summer you asked me to take some pictures for you at camp this year because you couldn't be there," James explained. "Well, I didn't exactly take pictures." James opened my DVD player and put in a disk. "I hope you like this." Camp pictures, video clips, and memories scrolled across the screen. There was video of campers Derek had had his first year when he worked in play camp. Those same kids were now in my group. I couldn't believe how old some of the photos were. Pictures of Gene and Julie, rec. leaders in teal shirts, campers who are now in high school. For the next ten minutes songs that we all shared and people we all grew up with made appearances on the screen. It was hard to take it all in, at least in the several minutes I had in a room filled with people. That video was a snapshot into the last six years of my life. It felt as if James pulled out that part of my memory and put it onto a DVD.

A few weeks later my teaching certificate arrived in the mail. The school year was here, so I hastily went to register with Chicago Public Schools. James and Joanne began their teaching careers, but I left the country. I had booked a flight to Italy to visit Keith for two weeks. On the plane I could not help but think, *the rest of my life is in front of me.*

When I arrived, Keith planned trips for us to see Rome, Venice, and Verona. We talked about Chicago most of the time. He was tired of being away from everyone, from the city, from his old life. I felt the same way about camp. The Park was just as much my home as the house I lived in.

When I returned home from Italy I was hoping to have a message from the Board of Education. My mailbox was empty and my voice mail was blank. No calls about my future life as a teacher. So, with no job and endless hours of free time, I decided to begin writing.

I sat around with camp and teaching constantly on my mind. I wrote and read and wrote some more. I wrote a story about my life. Six years during high school and college that shaped me into who I am today. How six summers and one place can just take control. Four months of writing went by and I still was not cleared to start teaching. Finally, over winter break, I was cleared to work and got hired as a full time substitute teacher at my old grade school. Six summers of camp and an entire lifetime of experience was finally ready to be utilized.

James is currently teaching seventh grade English in a suburb of Chicago. He and Joanne just celebrated their four-year anniversary.

Derek graduated with a degree in journalism from the University of Arizona. He returned to Chicago where he lives with Megan and works as a dog walker.

Caitlin and I are still dating. She is working on her teaching degree at Northeastern Illinois University and works year round at The Park.

Cesar was hired as an athletic trainer for the Cincinnati Reds single-A farm team. He travels with the team every summer and lives in Chicago every winter. We're still friends.

Nick drives into the city every few of weeks to visit. We are still close today.

Big White went to Iraq in 2006. He returned unharmed to his base in Georgia and has visited Chicago a few times. I have not seen him in over a year.

Butthole is working his way through high school. He skateboards regularly and thinks he is in love. I see him every summer when he stops by The Park. We remain friends today.

Leslie transferred out of U of I sophomore year. I have not talked to her since.

Dale is half way through college at Illinois State University. He plans on working at The Park next summer.

So do I.

Printed in the United States
123812LV00001B/95/P

9 781598 584127